'Having faith is having hope, and hope helps us to dispel our fears and to channel our energy into what we can be hopeful for. Katie Piper is a symbol of hope who inspires us to believe that things can get better, no matter how hard we are challenged. She reminds us to have faith.'
Kamran Bedi, life coach and author

'Katie is THE example of a positive, uplifting human being. Her daily affirmations on social media are always so encouraging, so to have them all in one book is such a great idea and will help so many.'
Olivia Bowen, TV personality

'Katie Piper is a sheer force for good, embodying great strength, resilience, determination and hope. Katie has unflinchingly shared her experiences and the life lessons she's garnered over the years with her million-strong community, helping them to feel inspired and empowered. Her wise and nourishing daily mantras within this book will provide you too with the courage to transform your life, and it couldn't come at a more poignant or apt time.'
Vicki Broadbent, founder of Honestmum.com, bestselling author of *Mumboss* and TV broadcaster

'Katie Piper is such an empowering person. Anyone who has struggled with adversity and fought their way out of tough situations can take comfort and inspiration from her approach to life.'
Matt Haig, author

'Katie embodies strength, resilience and positivity, and that is truly reflected in her new book. If you're in need of something to lift you up and fill you with confidence, then this book is for you.'
Alice Liveing, personal trainer, author and Instagrammer

'Katie is such a shining light and positive role model for so many, including me. This book will uplift readers with her advice, positivity and spirituality.'
Andrea McLean, TV presenter and *Sunday Times* bestselling author

'Katie personifies all the traits I most admire in people: courage, resilience, determination, mental strength, a refusal to do self-pity, and a fantastically positive and optimistic view of life whatever hurdles are put in her way.'
Piers Morgan, broadcaster, journalist, writer and television personality

'Faith, positivity and spirituality can be such powerful tools in life. No one epitomizes them more than Katie Piper. A wonderful, uplifting book and guide for those who need daily guidance and light in their lives.'
Louise Pentland, author, YouTuber and UN ambassador

'In a world that often feels designed to prevent recovery from trauma, Katie Piper is the inspirational warrior we all need. A champion of how to survive and then thrive no matter what tragedy life sends our way. Katie Piper is someone we admire greatly and we often look to her for positive words and affirmations to pick us up.'
Ian Redpath and Jeremy Chopra, authors of *All on the Board*

'Katie's zest for life is a tonic for the soul.'
Susanna Reid, TV presenter

'Katie personifies heart, courage, endurance and hope as the extraordinary woman she is. It is beautifully expressed in this gift of a book that every one of us can learn and grow from.'
Julia Samuel, bestselling author, speaker and psychotherapist

'Faith, positivity and spirituality can be such powerful tools in life. No one epitomizes this more than Katie Piper does.'
Nadia Sawalha, TV presenter and personality

'Katie is one of the most uplifting souls I've come across – online and offline. One minute in her company and you feel anchored by her beautiful rawness and extraordinary energy. To have 365 days of her thoughts in one book is the tonic everyone needs right now. It's like having a friend in a book.'
Anna Whitehouse, aka Mother Pukka – author, radio presenter and campaigner

'Katie has always been an inspiration to me. She is beautiful inside and out, and has devoted her life to helping and inspiring others, which shows how selfless and amazing she is. Her positivity shines through and her book is the perfect example of this.'
Jessica Wright, TV personality and businesswoman

'Katie radiates positivity! A book for those who need daily uplifting affirmations from one of the most inspiring women I know. A must-read to brighten up your days.'
Laura Whitmore, author and presenter

Katie Piper is a TV presenter, philanthropist and the bestselling author of several books.

Described as an 'icon of her generation', Katie secured her place in the nation's hearts when she appeared on Channel 4's BAFTA nominated documentary *Katie: My Beautiful Face*, which covered the early stages of her recovery after an acid attack in 2008. For more than a decade, Katie has devoted her life to the Katie Piper Foundation to support those living with burns and scars; she has received numerous awards, accolades and doctorates for her work.

Katie is a much-loved presenter for the BBC's *Songs of Praise* and for BBC Radio 2, the host of the acclaimed *Katie Piper's Extraordinary People* podcast and face of iconic global beauty brands. She is dedicated to removing the traditional stigma of beauty across the media and will continue to lead thought that promotes diversity, inclusion and acceptance across society.

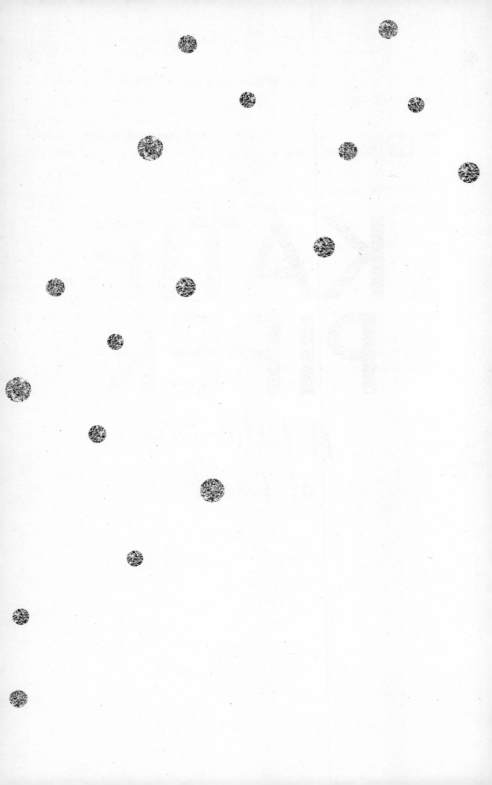

KATIE PIPER

A Little Bit of Faith

Hopeful affirmations
for every day of the year

First published in Great Britain in 2021

Society for Promoting Christian Knowledge
36 Causton Street
London SW1P 4ST
www.spck.org.uk

Text copyright © Katie Piper 2021
Illustrations copyright © Getty Images and © Creative Paper via Creative Market

Scripture quotations are taken from The Holy Bible, New International Version
(Anglicized edition). Copyright © 1979, 1984, 2011 by Biblica. Used by permission
of Hodder & Stoughton Ltd, an Hachette UK company. All rights reserved. 'NIV' is a
registered trademark of Biblica. UK trademark number 1448790.

British Library Cataloguing-in-Publication Data
A catalogue record for this book is available from the British Library

ISBN 978–0–281–08650–4
eBook ISBN 978–0–281–08649–8

Typeset by Fakenham Prepress Solutions, Fakenham Norfolk NR21 8NL
Printed and Bound in Great Britain by Clays

eBook by Fakenham Prepress Solutions, Fakenham Norfolk NR21 8NL

Produced on paper from sustainable forests

To my affirmation gang on Instagram – swapping quotes and sharing a love for these scribblings of hope and light in our lives mean the world to me. This one is for you x

Introduction

Those who keep up with me on social media will know how much I value affirmations. I've been reading these positive nuggets on my Instagram stories over the past year, partly to remind myself and partly to remind you how important it is for us to speak the right things over ourselves.

When it comes to affirming positive thoughts, I think we all know the sorts of statements we *should* be thinking and saying about our lives. In practice, though, it's often a different story. We're all too quick to allow the 'not good enough' tape to play. If we don't take positive action, so many of us can slip into telling ourselves 'I can't do this', 'I will mess up', 'I look terrible', 'They won't like me'. . .

That's why it's so important to have the truth written down, so when you don't feel it, you can look at the words to remind yourself. I believe that things sink in better when they are visual. It's clear from all this that it's not enough simply to know the positive quotes; we need to have them written down, see them and say them to ourselves on a daily basis to remind ourselves they are true.

Using affirmations has helped me to stay positive throughout my adult life. My hope is that this will be the same for you too. Use this book every day, in the morning or when you're about to turn the lights off in bed, or just dip in and out whenever you feel you need a quick injection of hope or confidence – there's no pressure, no right or wrong time, it's what works best for you. When you find something inspiring, always be sure to share it. Drop a photo of the page on your WhatsApp chat, post it on your social media or write it on a note and give it to someone who's been on your mind. You never know, that person may be having a really tough day and your support and solidarity could be just what he or she needs to keep going.

1

Introduction

As you read through these pages, you will notice that there's also an element of faith woven through the book. I'm not from a religious family but I became a believer in my twenties and I wrote about this journey in my first autobiography, *Beautiful*. Knowing that God has a plan for me has helped me to make sense of my life. I've been able to trust in him and it's allowed me to live a free life where fear doesn't hold me back. Faith is a very personal thing and whatever yours is, please know that you're welcome here.

I hope the words you are about to read set you free and give you the daily tools you need to strengthen your mindset and believe in yourself as you live the unique, beautiful life you were made for.

January

Today is the first blank page of a 365-page book. I'm going to write a good one.

If I'm honest, I'm not a huge resolutions person. I don't think you have to wait until 1 January to make a positive change in your life; any day is a good day to start again or start something new. But I have always found New Year's Day to be a great time to reflect on the amazing things that you have in your life and your hopes for the future. There is optimism in the air around this fresh starting point: the next year is a book of blank pages and you get to write your own story. So, what are your three biggest goals for the year ahead?

January

2 January

I will take time for myself today:
to pause, to pray, to meditate.

What it means to 'pray' and 'meditate' may take many different forms, depending on what you believe. It may be a moment of quiet reflection before your day. For me, I pray, but I don't pray in the traditional way, with my hands together or on my knees. I often pray in my head while walking around or running errands. Sometimes I say things out loud, as if I'm chatting to a mate. I write little notes and scribble in my journal. These things are valuable for your mind, whether you have a faith or not. I believe that everyone benefits from the sense of off-loading and feeling the peace and calm that come with meditation.

3 January

Nothing can stop you from letting go and making a fresh start.

When I see barriers in my path, I like to ask myself, 'Who put them there?' Through my own self-development and working with others over the years, I've found that the barriers we feel restricted by are often those we put in place ourselves. Have you created a barrier that's stopping you from being victorious? Do you need to reframe it?

4 January

There is wonder in everybody, and I will choose to look for it.

Look for the best in each person you meet and you will find it. I'm always blown away by the stories people have to share and the things that they've been through. There really is something miraculous and inspiring and incredible in each person's life. Take the time to listen to them and connect with them and I promise that you'll uncover some gold.

5 January

I will repeat things that I need to hear.

I am well aware that a lot of the messages in this book may be familiar to you already! I find, when I read affirmations, they're often ideas that I already know about or I've seen on social media before. That doesn't matter. The repetition and saying them out loud mean that they sink in a little bit further. Don't be afraid to repeat things over and over. I've found it so helpful in my journey to keep coming back to my favourite affirmations, just as a reminder!

6 January

If you can't change it, change the way you think about it.

Maya Angelou

(Wouldn't Take Nothing for My Journey Now, Random House, 1992)

We can try to focus on the good things in our lives and be genuinely grateful for them but, unfortunately, it won't stop bad things from happening. There will always be aspects of our lives or circumstances that we wish we could change but we just can't. In those times, I have to remind myself that some situations are just out of my control. Then I have to decide how I'm going to view that situation, trusting that things will unfold how they are meant to and I am growing as a consequence.

The greatest challenge in life is discovering who you are. The second greatest is being happy with what you find.

When I was younger, I definitely thought that I knew who I was. Now that I've had a few more years of working things out, I realize that, back then, I knew nothing! I'm sure that in twenty years' time I'll look back at me now and feel the same way. Life is a daily opportunity to learn more about ourselves but, alongside that, we need to learn to love ourselves as we are. Having grace for yourself and your flaws is often the place to start. We're never going to be perfect, but we are doing our best and we *are* worthy of love.

8 January

Every time I thought I was being rejected for something good, I was actually being redirected to something better.

Steve Maraboli

(*Unapologetically You*, Better Today, 2013)

The ultimate trust in God or a spiritual higher power is in saying, 'I surrender. I can't understand why this is happening to me, but I will have faith in the idea that this thing I wanted wasn't right for me.' In my life, even if I have really desperately wanted something to happen, I have learnt to accept that there was a different and hopefully better outcome for me.

I will not focus on pleasing others.

Something I've learnt over the years is that, if you set your life up to please your parents or to appease a romantic partner, it's only you who suffers. I've found that it can be so easy to lose your sense of your own identity if you put what pleases others before what pleases you. It's far better to focus on what brings you joy, peace and hope for the future! What things in your life are a source of joy and contentment for you today?

10 January

Doubt kills more dreams than failure ever will.

Suzy Kassem

(*Rise Up and Salute the Sun*, Awakened Press, 2011)

You may or may not fail when you try something new, that's a fact of life. In reality, failure isn't scary, it helps us grow. Failing itself doesn't have to kill a dream; it may just help you refine it so that you can come at it from a different angle. What is just as important as not worrying about failing? Not doubting yourself. I know that failure is possible, but I don't doubt that I can cope with it if it comes and can build something even better after the experience.

Do an act of kindness: write a positive review of a local business.

I always try to leave online reviews for small businesses if they've given me good service. If I haven't enjoyed something, I don't write a review at all – just in case it was a one off or they were having a bad day. It costs us nothing to champion business owners and it only takes a minute or two. Who could you write a positive review for today?

12 January

I will let my faith be bigger than my fear.

We can all feel anxious and afraid about the future. I love the idea, though, of not ignoring the fear but choosing to rise above it instead. So rather than getting rid of the fear or pretending it's not there, we can just keep reminding ourselves that our faith is bigger. I love thinking that we can overcome it not by fighting the fear down but by building our faith up.

Being happy doesn't mean that everything is perfect. It simply means that you've decided to look beyond the imperfections.

Attributed to Gerard Way

Constantly striving for the perfect set-up, material things, job or life has never led to happiness for me. When I look around at the people who are most content, they're often not the ones who have the most, but they're the ones making the most of what they have. I don't think 'perfect' exists any more. There's no argument-free relationship or flawless house or immaculately behaved children (at least not that I've discovered!). There are just people getting by, choosing to enjoy the cards they've been dealt and cultivating their contentment.

14 January

I will do my bit to make the world a better place.

Sometimes I feel that everyone is trying to build the best lives for themselves alone. The more I think about it, though, the more I feel doing that is a waste of time. If we focus outwards instead, on developing a kind world with a culture of understanding that upholds human dignity, we will all have a better place to live and all our lives will be greatly improved as a result.

For the LORD your God is the one who goes with you to fight for you against your enemies to give you victory.

Deuteronomy 20.4

I know this won't ring true for everyone, particularly if you're not a Christian, but I've included it because the idea of knowing that God is on my side is a big deal for me. It means I don't feel down when I hit a wall or when someone pushes back on something I say or do. It's a comfort to know that I'm supported regardless, and I don't fight my battles alone.

16 January

Act as if what you do makes a difference . . . it does.

William James

(*The Will to Believe and Other Essays in Popular Philosophy*, Cambridge University Press, 2014)

We can all fall into the trap of feeling we're not that important and what we do doesn't make a difference in the world. You may not be prime minister or winner of the Nobel Peace Prize, but what you do does actually make a difference. Every kind word you offer and smile you give will make a difference to those people – they could even change their lives. Never underestimate your impact!

Comparison is the fastest way to feel unhappy.

I know many people may think that comparison arrived with the advent of social media, but I for one remember it being a factor long before Instagram! I can remember my friends and I comparing our looks or skin or body sizes ages ago. The fact is, even if we all read the same things and used the same creams and ate the same food and exercised the same amount, we'd all end up looking totally different from one another. We're not in competition with others and seeking to be is destructive. Is there someone you could stop comparing yourself to today?

18 January

One of the hardest lessons in life is letting go. Whether it's guilt, anger, love, loss or betrayal, change is never easy.

Attributed to Mareez Reyes

When we allow ourselves to get wrapped up in heavy feelings, they can start to define us. If such negative thoughts get too engrained, we can get comfortable with them and that makes it so hard to break free of these patterns of thinking and the feelings that follow. Don't get me wrong, I experience strong emotions from time to time – we all do! – but for me it's important not to let them take over. Is there a strong emotion that you've needed to journey through but have begun to dwell in that you could begin to let go of today?

19 January

Those who follow the crowd usually get lost in it.

Rick Warren

(*The Purpose Driven Life*, Zondervan, 2009)

At different times in my life, I've both followed the crowd and decided to follow my own path. Not being able to blend in with the masses has turned out to be one of my biggest strengths. It took some time, but now I am able to do my own thing and make the decision that feels right for me – not for everybody else.

20 January

You don't have to see the whole staircase, just take the first step.

Martin Luther King Jr

(M. Marable and L. Mullings (eds), *Let Nobody Turn Us Around*, Rowman & Littlefield, 2003)

I know that when you're anxious, doing anything without a guaranteed outcome is a huge challenge. We all want to know how the journey will end when we set out. I understand that I'm never going to know the story from start to finish so, for me, I draw on my faith to keep me going. Believing that I'm being looked out for, and that there is a plan for my life, means I don't feel so scared when I take that first step. Is there a step forwards that you could take today but have been putting off because you don't know what the outcome will be?

Excellence is a value; perfectionism is an insecurity.

I don't know about you, but I can be my own worst critic at times! I'm competitive and I hate feeling that I messed something up – even when it's the 'messing up' that can teach me the biggest lessons. I have to be strict with myself and draw a line between striving to do things well and striving for perfection. We will always fall short of perfection and that's OK – we're human, with all the beauty and brokenness that comes with it.

22 January

But that inadequacy or feeling of inadequacy never really goes away; you just have to trudge ahead in the rain regardless.

Attributed to Lorrie Moore

Absolutely everyone will feel that they're not good enough every now and again. That doesn't mean they're crippled by it but, from time to time, it will crop up. I know when I had my first baby, I suffered massively from imposter syndrome. I didn't know what I was doing at all, but then I settled into it. When I went back to work, I had imposter syndrome all over again, as I thought I'd forgotten everything! The fact is, you are equipped and ready to deal with what's in front of you — even if it doesn't always feel that way.

I will not play it small when I was made to live life in all its fullness.

The options we have in life are so endless. I think I really started living life to its fullest when I found my passion for and my purpose in what I do. This discovery also came with risk. I had to run the risk that I would fail. Every time I put myself out there to try to achieve my dreams, I faced the possibility of rejection. That's tough, but when it's in service of your passion, every part of it feels worth it.

January

24 January

I'm rewriting my story and it's beautiful.

There's something I used to do when I was wrestling with my circumstances that would really help me. I used to picture my life as if it were a film, but in my film, I wasn't just the lead actor; I was the producer and director as well. That meant, when there were scenes in the film that were challenging, I could direct and produce how short the scene was going to be. I could decide that that scene would just be a moment and I could make the following, more positive, scenes much longer. Plus, the biggest bonus was that I got to play my part in writing the ending. How can you step into your leading role today?

25 January

I will give thanks to you, LORD, with all my heart; I will tell of all your wonderful deeds.

Psalm 9.1

Religious or not, this feels like such a wonderful message of positivity! No matter what you believe in, it's so important to give thanks and recognize the wonderful deeds around us. I always like to try to start the morning with a thankful heart and look out for all the good things people do and say as I go about my day. Perhaps tomorrow you can look back and be thankful for things that happened today.

26 January

Some days, there won't be a song in your heart. Sing anyway.

Emory Austin

There are plenty of lovely, encouraging quotes in this book, and I do mean what I say, but I am also a realist. We can talk about being positive and making the most of life all we want, but sometimes we just don't feel up to it, and that's OK. If you're in that place today, don't let it dampen your spirit. Not every day will be a good day. If you possibly can, sing anyway, but if you can't, don't worry; the song will still be waiting for you tomorrow.

I will not let the disappointments of today keep me from pursuing my dream tomorrow.

It would be such a shame to let something upsetting ruin how you feel about your future. Even if something difficult hits, you're still you. You still have your hopes, dreams and aspirations. To carry the doubts and disappointments of yesterday into today is really giving power or control to that person or issue. What can you leave behind today?

Going through pain will make me wiser.

There's so much wisdom to gain from anyone who has really battled through something. I think it's sad that we're moving into an era when there won't be anyone alive who fought in the First and Second World Wars. Any time I hear those who have speak in an interview or I read about their stories, I'm always struck by the incredible wisdom and perspective these people have on life. How can looking back on other people's times of hardship and victories in books, films and documentaries help us as we move forwards?

Resentment is like drinking poison and waiting for the other person to die.

Attributed to Carrie Fisher

In my experience, if you let resentments fester, it only affects you. They can start to infect your attitude and your thinking and, ultimately, your happiness. If you stay angry with somebody, who are you punishing? Is there a resentment you could let go of today?

30 January

When I feel weak and inadequate, I will lean into love and live fully.

I don't know what love – at its fullest – means to you, but the Bible says that God *is* love. For me personally, I believe that God knows and understands me fully, which means he also knows when I'm doubtful and feeling a bit lost. When I've been in that place, I've always felt that he's there to pick me up. Resting in the comfort of knowing that he has enough strength for both of us gives me the confidence to keep going and fully embrace life.

31 January

I will challenge myself.

Some of the affirmations in this book will suggest a way forward or a change of mindset, but sometimes I think that a good affirmation leads us instead to think more deeply about something and come to our own conclusions. Are there any of the affirmations you have already read that you could go back to and challenge yourself to think about in more depth? Is there anything you brushed over because it 'felt too hard' when you first read it? You have the power to challenge yourself and change. We are often more courageous than we first think.

February

Love is never wrong.

People feeling, showing and acting out of love is so beautiful. It warms my heart when I see any display of love around me. I champion all types of love and the beauty that comes from them all. Who could you show more love to today?

2 February

I will allow myself to change, progress and grow.

As you will, no doubt, have picked up on by now, I see life as being a bit like a book. There are lots of different chapters and it's healthy for you to move through them. Sometimes closing a chapter will mean a change in your social circle, lifestyle or even your own character and that's OK. Sometimes it's time to turn the page, so don't be afraid to do so!

3 February

I will keep things in perspective.

I find it helpful to take a look at problems for what they really are and not what I've built them up to be in my head. I know this technique isn't for everyone, but I break a situation down and ask myself what the worst outcome would be for each scenario. I find that this gives me a better perspective on the situation and reminds me what's important.

4 February

Be strong enough to walk away from those who continue to hurt you. Be brave enough to walk alone until you find the one who deserves you.

Unknown

I've had my fair share of bad relationships over the years, and I've learnt that it really is better to tackle things on your own rather than with someone who doesn't have your best interests at heart. Being alone, in the romantic sense, doesn't mean that you have to be lonely. You can spend time with friends, family or with people in your community. You don't need to lean on one person who isn't right for you when you have an army of people ready to lift you up.

I will recognize and not question my capabilities.

We are capable of so much more than we believe! I often look at a task and it can feel so out of my comfort zone. Sometimes my first thought is not to try, because I think I can't do it. But then my second thought is that I've felt this way before and I've always been able to overcome and do the tasks. By reminding myself what I'm capable of, I can simply get on with it!

6 February

There is . . . a time to be silent and a time to speak . . .

Ecclesiastes 3.7

We have become a nation obsessed with talking and asking others for answers. Sometimes it's important to speak up, but sometimes you can learn everything you need to know simply by observing. I've often found the wisest person in the room is the quietest.

I don't need to diminish my problems by thinking that there is always someone worse off than me.

It is important to keep your problems in perspective but, at the same time, telling yourself that you don't have the right to feel upset will never make you feel better. I find the best thing to do is acknowledge where you're at and allow yourself to feel it, without bothering with comparison. Once you've acknowledged pain, you can find a way to soothe it and move on.

8 February

I will get up. I've not lost everything while I still have my life.

If simply getting up each day feels like a struggle, I'm sorry that is the case for you right now. Sadly, you are not alone in this – a number of other people will also relate to needing to speak these words over themselves. I know how it feels to be low and worried about what you've got left in your life. Even if you don't feel it today, know that there is hope for you. There is plenty in your life to make it worth getting up and dusting yourself off again. You can do this!

Fall in love with somebody who will never let you go to sleep wondering if you still matter.

Particularly when I was younger, I used to fall into the trap of going for the guy who kept me on my toes. As I've got older, I've realized that to cause uncertainty in someone isn't a sign of attraction; it's just plain being mean. If someone doesn't realize your value and show it through consistent love, care and attention, then perhaps that person isn't the right one for you to have in your life.

10 February

Sometimes you have to let go of the past with acceptance, value the present with gratitude and anticipate the future with hope.

I don't know about you but, for me, letting go has been a challenge at times. I push myself to do it but it's not always easy. When we do allow ourselves to release our grasp on the past, it frees up our head space to truly enjoy what we have in the present and cultivate hope for the future. What one thing could you let go of or appreciate or look forward to today?

11 February

I will remember who I am and why I'm here. I'm never given anything in this world that I can't handle.

My faith is a large source of strength when it comes to tackling difficulties. When I'm up against a big trial, I believe that God doesn't allow me to go through anything that I can't withstand. It means that, even if it doesn't feel like it, I know I have the tools available to me to navigate the situation. Where do you draw your strength from in times of trouble?

February

12 February

Do an act of kindness: invite someone to stand in front of you in a queue.

We're always in such a big rush that when someone does something like offer for us to go next in the queue, it feels really special, especially as the gesture means giving up some time for us too. You never know, the person you let in could be stressed and pushed for time, so you might have just made their day.

Friendship isn't about who you've known the longest; it's about who walked into your life and said, 'I'm here for you' and proved it.

I don't know where I'd be without my friends but, as with everything in life, my friendships evolve and change as my circumstances do. It doesn't mean that my old friendships aren't important to me, but it may be that a more recent friendship provides more support for me in my current situation. We can often feel disloyal admitting that, but it's OK. Your old friends will have new friendships that they feel the same way about too!

14 February

I will be my own valentine.

Valentine's Day is about love, but that doesn't have to be love from a romantic partner. We are all entitled to love and be surrounded by love regardless of our relationship status! How about you don't wait for someone else to sweep you off your feet today but, instead, recognize that love is already in your life and celebrate that? Treat yourself to something nice, run a bath, eat some yummy food, care for yourself the way you deserve. You're so loved today and every day – don't forget that!

I am comfortable with who I am. In fact, I'm unapologetic about it.

It took me so long to feel comfortable in my own skin, but once I got there, I felt completely liberated. I think that this is particularly difficult as a woman, as how comfortable we feel is often associated with how we feel about our looks or our weight. Whenever I've pushed past any physical insecurities and embraced the person I am deep down, though, I have realized that I don't need to justify myself or conform. I am unapologetically me!

16 February

I will strive to understand those around me and give them a safe space to be themselves.

I've always felt that one of the key messages of Christianity is to show love to those around us. We shouldn't be seeking revenge or fighting fire with fire. Instead, we should be trying to understand people and offer them a safe space to express themselves. Often, I think, people are simply looking for a warm welcome and a listening ear.

17 February

Love looks outwards.

Having an outward-minded attitude and perspective has always been far more rewarding for me than looking inwards. I think the ultimate expression of love is putting the needs of someone else before my own. It also helps me not to be so focused on my own troubles, needs and successes but, instead, to see the world as a community where, ultimately, we're working towards a common good. How can you look outwards today?

February

18 February

There is surely a future hope for you, and your hope will not be cut off.

Proverbs 23.18

The fact that there is always hope is a huge comfort to me. I draw particular strength from the words 'future hope' in this ancient proverb. Sometimes we don't have the strength to hope in the moment, so it's reassuring to know that it's coming. If you're finding yourself without hope today, fix your eyes on the future and know that the best is yet to come.

Wanted: encouragers. We have a surplus of critics already. Thanks – The World

There is so much negativity and naysaying that it's great to be a voice of positivity. While 'realism' is important, a lot of people don't know how to be realistic without being miserable! There are good things all around us and it's wonderful to point them out. How can you be an encourager today?

20 February

The truth is still true even if no one believes it. A lie is still a lie even if everyone believes it to be true.

I feel so much peace when I think about the idea that people's perceptions can't change what is true. To me it means that truth always triumphs, no matter what. Often, I've found that it doesn't feel that way straight away but, in time, the truth always reveals itself. Resting in that idea means I don't have to waste energy trying to persuade people. I sleep easy knowing that they'll work it out for themselves eventually.

21 February

I don't have regrets. I did the best I could with what I had.

The truth is, regret doesn't serve any purpose. If you did something when you didn't know better, then it's just an opportunity to learn and improve for next time. By basking in the regrets of the past, you inhibit your future. Is there anything in your past that you find it difficult to move on from? How could you take positive steps to let go of regrets today?

22 February

Courage doesn't always roar. Sometimes courage is the quiet voice at the end of the day saying (whispering), 'I will try again tomorrow.'

Mary Anne Radmacher

We shouldn't confuse courage with being loud and ballsy. Sometimes it's the people who silently keep going, day after day, challenge after challenge, who are the bravest of all. When things haven't gone your way, look at the next day and see it as a chance to have another go. Just waking up and trying again is inspiring in itself.

There is a bigger plan for me than I have for myself.

I know this might sound a bit as though I'm palming off the important things, but I love the idea that I can shed responsibility for my direction in life and leave it to God! For others, this 'meant to be' mentality can be found in a different higher power or deep inside themselves. For me personally, I trust that God's plan for me is greater than anything I could dream up myself, so why not let him take the reins?!

24 February

I will love fearlessly today.

I believe that to love fearlessly is to be truly honest and vulnerable with how you feel. There is great risk in giving love so freely and it's important to remember that love and pain often go hand in hand. Even when you love the right person, there will be upsets and disappointment along the way, but don't let that stop you from loving with all your heart. The reward is always worth the risk, even if it doesn't look how you first imagined it.

25 February

I will spread joy online.

I've had my fair share of nasty messages online – the Internet can be a really horrible place. While some of those messages can hurt, I've learnt to remind myself that those people must be in real pain to speak to someone they don't know like that. I know that it's about them and not me. We can all counteract the negativity by writing a positive comment to someone on social media today. Who could you message to say how well they're doing or how much you admire their work?

26 February

Never hate jealous people. They're jealous because they think you're better than them.

Paulo Coelho

Feeling jealous is something that we all experience from time to time. The best thing is to acknowledge it and move on, wishing the other person success and good things. When the jealousy takes root, that's when the resulting toxicity can be really damaging. I've always felt that envy is a symptom of a lack of appreciation of our own uniqueness and self-worth. Each of us has something to give that no one else has, so don't spend time wanting someone else's gift. Embrace your own!

Sometimes the best way to appreciate something is to be without it for a while.

We can all have too much of a good thing from time to time. When you don't have it and then have it again, it's like when you're really hungry and you haven't eaten for a while, you appreciate that first bite so much more. Sometimes, the same applies for other good things in our lives. Perhaps you and your partner would benefit from spending the weekend apart? Maybe you'd enjoy your job again after a two-week holiday? Is there anything that you might appreciate a little more after some distance from it? How can you take steps to make this 'fast' or 'break' happen?

February

28 February

Faith is to believe what you do not see; the reward of your faith is to see what you believe.

Saint Augustine

Sermons, 4.11

When I first came to faith, I knew I was believing something that I would never be able to prove or see with my own eyes, but when people ask me about it, I just explain that I don't *have* to see it. Believing it does so much for me and I receive so much from walking out my faith in day-to-day life. I don't mind if other people don't share my viewpoint or feel that they need more proof. We all have to take our own journey.

An extra leap!

I will make time to go the extra mile today – for myself or someone else.

How many of us wish that we could have more hours in the day or an extra day in the week? In busy seasons of life, it can often feel as if time is slipping away from us but, often, it's all about priorities. Even so, every four years we get the gift of an extra day and, whether you're reading this affirmation in a leap year or not, why don't you prioritize something that always seems to slip off your to-do list, whether that's spending some time reading a book, having a bath or ringing a friend for a much-needed catch-up?

March

1 March

Spring brings new growth. Weed out the bad and make room for something beautiful.

When spring arrives and the days get just that bit longer, I start to look around for little signs of new life. Maybe that's me getting old! I love to see a daffodil poke up or leaves begin to grow on the trees again. The change of weather and the hints of growth help me to feel fresh and that life is full of possibilities. I think we can all feel our mood lifted as the days get brighter. Take a look at the world today and see if you can spot signs of new life. Maybe that can be your motivation to head positively into the coming season.

March

2 March

To exist is to change, to change is to mature, to mature is to go on creating oneself endlessly.

Henri Bergson

(A. Mitchell, C. Brereton, E. E. Slosson and F. L. Pogson (trans.),
The Essential Works of Henri Bergson, e-artnow, 2018)

This is a powerful affirmation, but I see it almost like a beautiful poem too. I think we all need to be reminded of this from time to time, that life will change and we need to roll with it. Far from being a weakness, the creative opportunities offered as life changes and we mature are endless. It also reminds me that maturity isn't about age; it's about mindset and experiences.

Do an act of kindness: give someone your seat on the bus or train.

Giving up your seat on the bus or train is thought of as a pretty old-fashioned thing to do these days. Rather than it just being men giving up their seat for women in black-and-white films, though, maybe we can all make way for someone else today. Whether they're old or with a child or just look as if they've done a hard day's work, they might really appreciate the offer.

4 March

I will not chase short-term fixes to long-term problems.

We can all look for comfort in the wrong places. Goodness knows, I've tried all kinds of things to patch things up in the past! I've now learnt that embracing and acknowledging hardship will mean that I move through it so much faster than I will if I give in to a, seemingly, quick fix. Don't distract yourself from difficult things. No situation will actually be made better by alcohol, drugs, sex, betting, overeating or any other damaging coping mechanism. How can you sit with your feelings today?

When you know you are great, you have no reason to hate.

There's a part of me that thinks announcing you're great is a little arrogant, but then another part of me thinks, 'No! We're so quick to point out our flaws that we should be able to stand up and say we're great!' Over time, I've learnt that when I recognize the amazing gifts in my life, I don't feel the need to dislike others around me for theirs. When was the last time you reminded yourself that you're great?

6 March

Peace I leave with you; my peace I give you. I do not give to you as the world gives. Do not let your hearts be troubled and do not be afraid.

John 14.27

I don't know if you're familiar with this verse from the Bible, but I'm so comforted by the idea that God leaves his peace for me. I've found it's so easy to get caught up in that anxious feeling in your tummy when something isn't going well and allow it to consume you with worry, but the fact that God sees troubled hearts and doesn't want us to be scared reassures me so much in difficult times.

7 March

Life is too short to be spent at war with yourself.

In an ideal world, we would be our own ally, cheerleader and friend. In real life, though, I know that I can be my harshest critic and worst companion! Far from being nasty to those around us, we can hold the biggest grudges against ourselves. In the end, who is that anger helping? Definitely not us. Is there something that you could forgive yourself for today?

When we speak, we're afraid that our words won't be heard or welcomed, but when we're silent, we're still afraid, so it's better to speak up and use our voices.

I know how easy it is to feel scared to raise your voice, particularly if you think your words will be twisted or misunderstood but, ultimately, to stay silent is more damaging. There are plenty of people who don't have the luxury of free speech around the world so, if we have the ability to, we can speak up for them. We can challenge injustice and stand up for what we believe is right. How can you use your voice today?

9 March

Enjoy the little things, for one day you may look back and realize they were the big things.

Robert Brault

('Quotable quotes', *Reader's Digest*, September 1986, p. 139)

For me, this affirmation really hit home during lockdowns brought on by the global pandemic. So much of my time before was focused on work and what I thought of as the 'big things', but then as work wound down and there was less to do, I started focusing on the 'small things', like the little moments with my family or a nice phone call with a friend. In the end, I've found that the most special things aren't the big trips or achievements; they're the small, daily habits and rituals you develop with the people you love.

10 March

Become so confident in who you are that no one's opinion, rejection or behaviour can rock you.

I've had to work really hard to make sure that my confidence levels aren't related to how accepted I feel by others. It's tough to stop other people's opinions swaying how I feel about myself, but it's been such a valuable thing for me to invest in. Ideally, we all want to be unshakable and completely immune to outside influence. In reality, it's not that simple, but we can at least be working towards a strong sense of self that will not be moved off track by other people's storms.

11 March

You will not always be strong but you can always be brave.

Attributed to Beau Taplin

I think it's important to remember that, while we all want to be strong, there are times when we aren't able to muster it. Keeping positive and making good decisions for ourselves doesn't mean that we'll be skipping through a life of joy. No one is strong all the time and it's a relief to acknowledge that, but bravery is accessible to us all.

12 March

Your prayer for someone may or may not change them but it always changes you.

Craig Groeschel

It's lovely to be thinking of others and praying for them but, actually, we can never influence the outcome of our prayers. That person may or may not change, but when we put others' needs front and centre in our lives, we definitely do. Reaching out and asking for help for someone helps me to put my life into perspective. It's healing for ourselves to put selfishness to one side and focus on someone else.

13 March

Caring for others is an expression of what it means to be fully human.

Hillary Clinton

(Remarks made when Secretary of State in recognition of International Human Rights Day, Palais de Nations, Geneva, 6 December 2011)

In the media, we continually see people with so much doing so little to care for others. I fully believe that selfishness chips away at an individual's humanity and that's why we can often see such people beginning to do worse and worse things. For me, caring for other people, whether my family, friends or people I meet through my charity the Katie Piper Foundation, allows me to interact with those individuals on a deep level and it is that connection and caring for others which is a vital part of being human.

14 March

Sometimes the worst place you can be is in your own head.

Our minds are powerful; they can be our biggest creator but also our biggest torturer. When it feels as if my thoughts are running away with me, that's when I call on my friends to help me out. The fact that we can be our own worst enemy is why we need those real connections in our lives. My friends will often help me to rationalize the thoughts that are causing me distress and encourage me to find healthy ways to decompress. What healthy action could you take to relieve some of the stress in your head? Maybe today is the day to set aside an hour for walking, exercise or a hobby or craft?

15 March

I will recognize whose shame it is to carry.

Sadly, it seems to me that the weight-loss industry trades in shame. It's become profitable to shame people, particularly women, who don't have the perfect body into buying shapewear products, detox teas and all manner of other things. Often, as women in society, we're controlled through shame. It's become a powerful tool. Who should really be ashamed? The mum-of-three who doesn't have the 'perfect bikini body' or the big company trying to use that to manipulate her into spending money?

16 March

Stop cheating on your future with your past. It's over.

No one likes a cheater! All jokes aside, your future is where your focus should be now. It can be a bit like a relationship with an ex: we can reminisce and think about what we could have done differently when, really, we have so much ahead of us. Is there something in your past that you could move on from today, in order to fully invest in your future?

17 March

Luck is believing you're lucky.

Tennessee Williams

(*A Streetcar Named Desire*, New American Library, 1947, Scene Eleven)

There's a lot of talk about being lucky around St Patrick's Day and it's all good fun, but being lucky isn't what's really important. Hard work and believing in your capabilities is what brings the success we can sometimes fall into the trap of seeing as 'luck'. Don't worry about being lucky; worry about knowing that you are worthy of good things and can work towards them, because that's all 'luck' really is!

18 March

He who was seated on the throne said, 'I am making everything new!' Then he said, 'Write this down, for these words are trustworthy and true.'

Revelation 21.5

For me, there's so much reassurance in the idea that God is making everything new. It means I don't feel weighed down when I realize that I'm getting things wrong, because I believe that God's aim is to restore us and work with us so we become new people.

19 March

Life is 10 per cent what happens to you and 90 per cent how you react to it.

Charles R. Swindoll

I've tried to stay away from some of the better-known, clichéd affirmations that you will have seen or heard before, but when I reread this one, I couldn't resist! Sometimes it's popular because it's true. If you're in a place where you're not sure why things are happening around you, it's important to remember what's in your control. You probably can't change the actual event, but you can make sure that you represent yourself well in the way you respond. How could you respond to a situation today in a way that makes you feel proud?

March

Do an act of kindness: bake your favourite recipe and drop it off with someone who has a lot going on at the moment (or just buy something nice if you don't have time).

Cooking for someone shows that you've really set aside the time to do something especially for them. Plus, I find baking can be quite a meditative thing to do, so you could benefit from the calming effects of doing a nice thing too. Maybe there's someone who's not often thought of who would be really touched by the gesture? It could be the first time in months someone has done something kind for them. Never underestimate your impact!

I will pursue something that gives me fulfilment.

I love to work hard and it's obviously important for me and my family that I am paid for that work, but I get so much more from my job than money. I find the voluntary work I do with my charitable foundation so fulfilling that I would never give it up. I know some of us don't have the luxury of combining our jobs with our passions, but it is important that we feel fulfilled. Maybe for you that could mean a career change, volunteering for a charity or even simply taking up a new creative hobby!

22 March

Confidence is silent.
Insecurities are loud.

I think a lot of us assume that the loudest person in the room is the most confident, but when you scratch beneath the surface, often those people are the most fragile and insecure. It's easy for people to feel that if they're brash and loud, they're protected and they can use that behaviour as a wall. If you're a person who does that from time to time, please know that you're enough and you don't need to perform. If, alternatively, you find yourself feeling frustrated with the loud, 'confident' people, just remember that all may not be as it seems.

The person who tries to keep everyone happy often ends up being the loneliest.

The sad fact is that if you bend over too far backwards for others, you'll end up in a situation where you're being used by people who don't have your best interests at heart. A good friendship is usually a 50/50 balance – maybe not every day and in every season, but largely overall. You should pick each other up and support each other equally. That means you'll avoid resenting those around you and you'll find the ones who really value you.

24 March

I want to live, not just survive.

There are times when I've felt that I'm just getting by, from one day to the next. I certainly slipped into that when we were all in the first lockdown during the COVID-19 pandemic. I don't think that we need to beat ourselves up for having days like that, but it shouldn't be our whole lives. We're not here just for the sake of being here; we're here to live life to its absolute fullest. How can you thrive today? What can you do to live to the fullest?

25 March

If you're feeling inadequate, worthless or not enough, you didn't get those ideas from God.

Lisa Bevere

(Twitter, 8 July 2020)

I guess, for me, this affirmation reminds me that those feelings of worthlessness we can all feel from time to time don't come from a good place. It reminds me not to trust them. Whether you believe in God or not, I hope you will agree that we shouldn't add more value to negativity. It's not right or good or fair. Do you have those feelings about yourself today? Maybe you could remind yourself that they're simply not true so you don't need to believe them!

26 March

Rejection is not someone wanting me out of his or her life; rejection is someone God wanted out of my future.

Rejection is always painful, whether that's in your professional or personal life, but it doesn't mean you weren't enough, even if it can feel that way. It's so important to unpick that belief. If you don't, it can really sink in. I know that, in the past, I've driven myself crazy asking, 'What could I have done differently?', but now I know that rejection is often more about the other person than it is about me.

I will remember that hurt people hurt other people.

It's important to remember that what happens to you at the hands of other people isn't about you; it's about them and the issues and struggles that they are dealing with. The fact is, even in the face of frustration, a person who is well balanced and in a good place won't lash out with angry words or aggressive behaviour. When you understand that hurt people hurt other people, you can develop a new level of empathy and say, 'I can't imagine the pain that person must be feeling to behave like that.'

28 March

Keep your lives free from the love of money and be content with what you have.

Hebrews 13.5

We all need money to get by – there's no point pretending that's not the case – but we don't have to live for it. I've found that when my decisions are driven by what will make me the most money, my lifestyle actually suffers rather than improves. Work hard to earn and provide for yourself and your loved ones, but don't let a love of money take over.

Spring: a lovely reminder of how beautiful change can truly be.

Unknown

We can all fear change, but one we all look forward to is spring. Maybe that's because it comes every year so it's not uncertain or scary for us! The beauty of the change all around us right now reminds me to embrace other types of change in my life. Rather than see it as a leap into the unknown, at this time of year it feels exciting – as if opportunity is everywhere!

30 March

Don't be afraid of change. You may lose something good, but you may gain something better.

I think, in society (or at least where I am in the UK), we're conditioned to be afraid of change. When I watch the David Attenborough nature documentaries, it's always the animals that adapt and evolve that survive best, so maybe we need to take a leaf out of their book! Having to update practices or reset our plans doesn't have to be scary. It could mean something even better is around the corner!

The mind is its own place, and in itself can make a heaven of hell, a hell of heaven.

John Milton

(*Paradise Lost*, Book 1, lines 232–3)

The fact is, our minds are capable of getting us out of a mess, but they're also the thing that can get us into a mess in the first place! They're so difficult to navigate. Getting the mindset balance right is not easy. I've learnt that I can't just sit in the cockpit and let my mind fly itself; I've got to make healthy choices to help my mindset and my thought-life stay on the right course. What wellness-positive decision could you make for your mindset today?

April

1 April

I don't need to suffer fools gladly.

Everyone has their annoying traits here and there. I know I can do things that wind up the people closest to me! There's a difference, though, between occasionally being a bit silly and someone who's wilfully misunderstanding you and constantly trying to wind you up. I like to surround myself with people who make me feel that I and my time are valuable to them. I choose to spend time with people who build me up and speak good things into my life!

2 April

Crying can bring relief, as long as you don't cry alone.

Anne Frank

It's important to know that crying doesn't mean you're failing to cope. It's not shameful to cry – in fact, it can be cathartic. If you can, reach out to a friend so you have someone to talk through with you how you're feeling. Is there anyone you could invite to support you while you cry?

My scars show strength, not weakness.

Whether you think of physical or mental scars when you read this, it's still true. I know that the scars we carry tell a story of what we've lived through, what we've survived and the strength we have coming out the other side. Don't hide your scars; wear them with pride!

4 April

I'm still far from being what I want to be, but with God's help I shall succeed.

Vincent van Gogh

(In a letter to his brother, Theo van Gogh, Isleworth, 26 August 1876)

I love the idea that someone as talented as the acclaimed artist Vincent van Gogh could recognize how much growing and developing he had to do. I think we all need to be humble and realize that, even though we're doing our best, we can still make further progress and that's OK. What area could you benefit from working on today?

5 April

Life doesn't get easier or more forgiving. We get stronger and more resilient.

Steve Maraboli

(*Life, the Truth, and Being Free*, Better Today Publishing, 2009)

Every stage of life comes with its own new challenges. In my life anyway, they haven't stopped coming as I've gotten older, but I do have far better coping techniques and I understand myself and my patterns better than I did when I was younger. I think I've stopped being dramatic when something goes wrong and I just know that I'll work it out and get through it.

6 April

I don't need someone to complete me; I only need someone to accept me completely.

I know that a lot of people holding this book won't have what they consider to be the perfect life. The fact is, nobody does – there's no one with an absolutely perfect life out there! When it comes to the people we care about, they will never be able to fix everything for us or 'make us whole', but that's good news rather than bad. We don't need to change everything we are; we just need to be accepted as we are. Who could you accept today, exactly as they are?

People will forget what you did, but people will not forget how you made them feel.

Attributed to Maya Angelou

This quote attributed to author and activist Maya Angelou really moves me as, in many ways, the sentiment of this affirmation is my hope for the whole book. I know that you may not remember individual affirmations, but I hope you'll take away a feeling of hope and peace as you look through these pages each day. I'd love it if you felt inspired to share the quotes and thoughts with people you care about. This isn't just a legacy I want to leave with you, but a legacy that I hope you can leave with others too. We can all leave a trail of positive breadcrumbs behind us each day!

Your perspective will either become your prison or your passport.

Steven Furtick

When it comes to those I work with through the charity, I'm always surprised that two people with very similar experiences can have completely different perspectives on what's happened to them. I'm even more surprised by how those perspectives can determine the outcomes of those experiences. Throughout my journey, I've found that every situation ends up being directed by our interpretation of it. How can you turn a difficult experience into your passport for travelling forwards positively?

9 April

Do an act of kindness: tell a friend that they're a great parent.

Many parents seem to think that they're doing a terrible job all the time! I wonder if it's all part and parcel of the guilt that comes with parenthood. Plus, communities of parents can feel a little shaming and judgemental at times. I can't think of a single parent who doesn't need to know how well they're doing, especially as children can be terrible at saying thank you!

10 April

Make every effort to keep the unity of the Spirit through the bond of peace.

Ephesians 4.3

This is a really special sentiment, as it highlights that in unity we find peace. Peace is such an important thing. When I'm not at peace, I can't concentrate on my work or enjoy spending time with my family because there's something dragging me down. To be given the gift of peace through unity is very special.

A clear rejection is better than a fake promise.

To hear a clear rejection is tough, but it's nowhere near as tough as being strung along. In life, there are a lot of fake promises and platitudes, but when someone speaks to me frankly and cuts through the fluff, I really appreciate it. If you're in a place to handle it, genuine feedback is really helpful. No one likes to waste their time and when someone is clear, you don't have to!

April

12 April

She was unstoppable, not because she didn't have failures or doubts but because she continued on despite them.

Beau Taplin

When I look at the people who inspire me, those I would consider 'my heroes' all have such visible weaknesses. I gain so much courage from seeing others who have overcome barriers when I am facing ones of my own. It doesn't mean that they had more skills or more courage than other people; it just means they chose to keep going anyway, which is incredible. To me, those people are unstoppable!

Overthinking is the art of creating problems that weren't there.

Overthinking is a trap we all fall into from time to time. For me, when something really matters, I can start to play out all the different scenarios that could happen in my head. Over the years, I've learnt that that worry is actually a waste of time. It just keeps your mind busy while achieving nothing productive at all. Is there something that you're overthinking today? Is it time to let it go?

April

14 April

Sometimes people try to expose what's wrong with you because they can't handle what's right about you.

When I can sense feelings of jealousy bubbling up in me, I know deep down that it's more about me than it is about the other person. I think if someone is overly critical about something in you, it's often because it's something they've struggled with or it relates to their own fears. Everyone has enough to be working out in their own life without pointing out someone else's flaws. Don't allow it to get you down!

The meaning of life is to find your gift. The purpose of life is to give it away.

Attributed to Pablo Picasso

Finding purpose can be a lifelong mission. What I've found is that when you're good at something, whether that be art, music, listening, reaching out or any other thing, you will never regret sharing it with others. How could your talents benefit someone else today?

Be a good person, but don't waste time trying to prove it.

The era of social media means that we are surrounded by performative 'good deeds'. Before the days of the Internet, it would have been considered crude to discuss the ways in which you were helping others or how much money you were donating to charity – that would make it more about you and less about the people you were trying to help. The fact is, if *you* know that you're doing a good thing, other people don't need to.

Don't tell your God how big the storm is; tell your storm how big your God is.

Regardless of what you put your faith in, I feel that this affirmation demonstrates how powerful we can be when we focus on the solution to our problems rather than the problems themselves. I know that when friends say to me that they're not doing so well and are feeling overwhelmed, I always say, 'But you're doing it! You're here right now, you're surviving!' I have found that the problem is never as big as we initially think. There's something bigger than it, and there's something bigger than us.

18 April

What you see and what you hear depends a great deal on where you're standing. It also depends on what sort of person you are.

C. S. Lewis

(*The Magician's Nephew*, The Bodley Head, 1955. © copyright CS Lewis Pte Ltd 1955. Reprinted with permission.)

I've had to decide, on multiple occasions, whether I'm going to be a positive or a negative person. I want to be a person who sees the best in a situation – even though sometimes that is a struggle! I'm also aware that our perspectives on a particular situation are affected by where we are in life, our finances and family and other things. Take the national lockdowns seen because of the global pandemic. If you loved the people you lived with and had a decent home with outside space, it wasn't that bad, but that wasn't everyone's story. I try to bear that in mind when problems arise.

One of the happiest moments in life is when you find the courage to let go of what you can't change.

I know that this is part of the prayer they say in addiction meetings: 'Grant me the serenity to accept the things I cannot change.' It's such a famous prayer because it's so important that all of us do this. I don't think it's just people in recovery from addiction who benefit from it. Knowing that we're not in control means that we can stop wasting our time trying to take charge. It's liberating!

20 April

Our deepest fear is not that we're inadequate. Our deepest fear is that we're powerful beyond measure.

Marianne Williamson

(*A Return to Love*, Harper Thorsons, 2015)

I first came across these words of Marianne Williamson when a woman wrote a really powerful letter to me. She had been born male, but felt that her external body didn't represent who she was inside. She spoke about not feeling comfortable with her outside appearance – something that I've definitely felt at times. It was such a beautiful message and I've treasured the note ever since. Whenever I think about my fears and hopes and dreams, I think about this quote and that letter. Let's embrace our power and share some encouragement with someone else today!

21 April

To cure jealousy is to see it for what it is; a dissatisfaction with self.

Joan Didion

I've realized that a lot of negative emotions are more about ourselves than the person they're directed towards. Don't shame yourself, though – we can all fall into a trap of feeing jealous. I know I have from time to time! The best thing we can do is ask ourselves why we're feeling that way – is it telling us that we would like to make a change in our own lives?

April

22 April

After you give so much of yourself to people over the years, one day you'll wake up and realize that you need someone to give to you too.

Sylvester McNutt III

It's not the fluffiest of realizations, I know, but it is true that if you continue to people-please and live for the approval of others, eventually you lose yourself. If you feel that you're so busy running around and giving to others that you don't make space for self-care in your life, perhaps you could make a change? If you relate to this, it could be time to look after you.

23 April

You cannot separate peace and freedom, because no one can be at peace unless he has his freedom.

Malcolm X

('Prospects for freedom' speech, 7 January 1965, New York, in G. Breitman (ed.), *Malcolm X Speaks*, Grove Weidenfeld, 1994)

I know that I am so fortunate to have a lot of freedom where I live, in the UK. If everything's going as it should, we have freedom of speech, freedom to move around as much as we like and freedom to practise whatever religion we like. For those who feel trapped, it's incredibly painful and they cannot feel at peace. When I think about the huge amount of freedom in my life, I don't think about the freedom to do as I please but, rather, the opportunity to do what is right. Could you stand up for somebody else's freedom today?

April

24 April

For where two or three gather in my name, there am I with them.

Matthew 18.20

Community is important and gathering together provides opportunities to develop that community and strengthen those bonds. It's something that was made so difficult during the pandemic and lockdown and so evidentially builds our faith when we come together. As a Christian, I love the power of congregating described in this verse. The idea that if we get together to pray or speak about our faith Jesus is with us and for us I find really reassuring.

This too shall pass.

I had a psychotherapist and author called Julia Samuels as a guest on my *Extraordinary People* podcast. She wrote a book called *This Too Shall Pass* (Penguin Life, 2021), exploring bereavement, but she wasn't just talking about death. She spoke about all sorts of things in our lives that come to an end. There are so many micro-bereavements we face and it's important to acknowledge that these can be really tough to wrestle with and journey through. One thing we can all hold on to is the simple fact that this too shall pass.

26 April

Success is the ability to go from one failure to another with no less enthusiasm.

Unknown

Whenever I read an affirmation like this, I always think of those successful businesspeople giving TED Talks and quoted on the covers of magazines. They always tell stories of falling flat on their face a million times before they picked themselves up again. If it's good enough for them and their fancy suits, why not for us too? We can keep going just like they did. They're not special — just persistent!

I will not judge others based on the small window on their life that I looked through.

Developing empathy is so important for us, for our own mental health, but also for the benefit of those around us and how we treat them. From all my research, I know that often negative behaviours are far more complex than they seem if we take them at face value. If someone hasn't behaved well, why not give them the benefit of the doubt? You don't know what has happened to cause them to act that way.

28 April

Do an act of kindness: leave a kind note for someone.

During the pandemic, there were loads of moving examples of various acts of kindness popping up on Facebook. One thing we did was create labels with positive words and short affirmations that we stuck on pebbles, then placed them along a path for people to find. We also made a little basket with friendly notes in it and put it by the door so that delivery drivers or anyone passing by could take one and be encouraged. Maybe you could leave a kind note for a stranger to find and brighten up their day? Perhaps drop a note to someone you know who's struggling?

29 April

Don't let something that's long gone continue to control you.

We can trap ourselves in so many cages. Our fear, our shame, our past – it can all box us in and make us feel that we're held captive. If something is gone and over, finding the emotional freedom we all need will feel like such an incredible release. After all, if we trapped ourselves, often we can take steps to free ourselves too.

30 April

Nothing can change God's love for you.

Sometimes it can feel as though I'm just getting everything wrong. I can convince myself that I'm a bad person and I don't deserve anything, but I now recognize that's the fear we develop as we experience rejection from other people. The quote is so reassuring when we feel like this as it shows there is no such thing as you going 'too far' in some way to be loved: God's love is limitless. Sometimes I have to remind myself of that.

May

1 May

Nothing is permanent.

This is one affirmation that I have repeated to myself constantly over the years. I know that, technically, there are things that can be permanent, like physical or emotional scars, but the way you feel about them won't last for ever. I felt a certain way about my scars 13 years ago, but now I feel very differently – they're just part of me now. That example alone has shown me how my mindset evolves and how difficult things won't feel difficult for ever.

2 May

Wise people are not always silent but they know when to be.

I can always spot the wise person in a meeting at work. They don't say a lot but when they do, it's well worth listening to. Being able to hold your tongue until it's really necessary is such a skill. I really admire those who have it. I'm working on being that person myself but it feels as if I'm a way off! Is there a situation today where you would be better off staying quiet, waiting to speak when it matters most?

A healthy mind does not speak ill of others.

When I'm in a good place, I find that not only do I not need to speak badly of others but also I actually don't even think those bad thoughts to start with. I don't get nearly so irritated by the people around me when I'm not stressed. It's when I've had a tough day or been struggling with something that I find my tolerance levels drop to zero! When you catch yourself thinking badly of someone else or even speaking badly about others, it's a good time to ask yourself, 'What's going on with me to make me think this way?'

Gratitude bestows reverence . . . changing for ever how we experience life and the world.

Attributed to John Milton

I've found that not taking things for granted is the biggest gift that I can give myself. It's been transformative because it means that I see so much of the good in the world instead of allowing my focus to settle on things that go badly. Grab a pen and paper and write down five things that you are most grateful for today!

Not every situation needs a reaction; some things are better left alone.

I reserve my energy for the people who I know are open to feedback and those I want to continue to grow a relationship with. If you're around someone and you don't particularly want to deepen your connection, why bother correcting them if they do something wrong? It will only cost you to challenge them and what would it achieve? You can't educate everyone. Instead, why not concentrate on the people you care about most?

May

Who of you by worrying can add a single hour to your life?

Luke 12.25

I've been known to worry about things too much, to let them fester in my head and infect my thoughts and steal my joy, but I've slowly learnt to believe this simple verse: what does worrying actually solve? The fact is, it solves nothing and can do nothing to improve or lengthen our lives. What are you allowing to steal your joy today?

7 May

I will push myself to progress.

There are elements of my work I focused on early in my career that I got so used to doing, they didn't feel like a challenge to me any more. I really felt that I wanted to progress my skills and learn new things. It was exciting for me to stop doing tasks (even if they did pay more money!) to focus on pushing forwards. Is there anything you do that's safe and isn't challenging you any more? Is it time to make a change?

I will gladly give.

At the Katie Piper Foundation, we rely on donations from other people to survive and do our work. I am always blown away by the generosity of our donors. Some of those who support us the most are not the richest in the world; they're just kind-hearted people who care about helping others. I've found that, in fact, giving to others benefits me greatly – it helps me not to be controlled by my money or my clothes or whatever material things I think I 'need' because, at times, I give them away and it is really freeing. Getting into that mindset was a brilliant shift for me. How might you be able to be generous with your time, your money or your resources today?

Envy is the art of counting the other fellow's blessings instead of your own.

Harold Coffin

I feel exhausted when I think about trying to keep up with some of the incredible women around me. I love it when I see their wonderful achievements, particularly because I know we're not competing. It was never my intention to apply for their job or fight their campaign or whatever else they've accomplished, so I don't need to be jealous of them. We all have our own path and I concentrate on mine and cheer others on along theirs. If I don't, it just distracts me from celebrating my own achievements!

Never let fear decide your future.

I have found so much freedom in not putting too much energy into the emotion of fear. For me, it's important not to let that invisible barrier stop me from making big decisions in my life. Fear can only go as deep as we allow it to. Don't let yourself dwell in anxiety over things that may never happen. What fear can you let go of today?

11 May

Don't let shame and guilt keep you any longer from receiving love.

I definitely used to think that my behaviour in my twenties meant that I couldn't connect with a church or be a Christian, even though I wanted to. I think I assumed that I would be judged and not accepted, but that was my own sense of shame playing tricks on me. The fact is, everyone is broken and has done things that they're not proud of, but it doesn't mean they can't receive love.

12 May

A secret to happiness is letting every situation be what it is and not what I think it should be.

When I think about embracing how things are, not trying to make them how I think they should be, I always think of that choice we have between being right and being happy. It can be frustrating to let situations play out and not course-correct, but I've found that taking a step back makes me far more relaxed and peaceful. What might you need to step back from today?

13 May

I will continue to believe that the best days are in front of me.

I don't think this necessarily means that every experience you have in the future will be better than the ones you have had in the past, but I do think that, as we get older, we learn how to find a deeper level of joy in things. I also think that we learn more about how difficult life can be, so we get greater enjoyment from the good things that we do experience. If you're going through a tough time now, remember that the best is yet to come and this hard place might help you enjoy the days ahead even more.

14 May

I will learn from those around me.

Every expert was a novice at some point and they learnt from those who went before them. We have a lot to learn from those who are older, wiser or more experienced than we are. I find so much value in listening to others. You never know, you may learn from their mistakes and save yourself some trouble too!

Don't use social media to impress people; use it to impact people.

Dave Willis

(Twitter, 24 August 2014)

We hear about the evils of social media all the time, and there's a lot not to like, but it's also such an incredible, far-reaching platform. When I think about the endless possibilities of social media, it seems sad that some confine their contributions to showing off. It's a global platform, enabling us to connect with many different cultures and countries, so we should use it for good. How can you use social media to experience something new today?

16 May

I am cared for by a love that will never leave me.

Even in some of my darkest times, I knew in my heart that God would never leave my side. I knew that I didn't have to go through it alone, because God was with me. Whether you consider yourself a spiritual person or not, I wonder if you've ever felt this way? At times, I felt that God was walking by my side, at others that he had gone ahead to clear the way and then sometimes it felt as though he was carrying me when I couldn't go on. Has there been a time in your life when you have felt similarly comforted and how can it help you feel confident today?

Do an act of kindness: champion someone on social media.

You just never know what kind of day someone is having, despite their cheerful social media update. That's why it's so encouraging when someone takes the time to praise another person publicly. It's a big pick-me-up for that person, but I always feel great too when I read those positive messages about other people. Who can you post an encouraging message about today?

Rejection doesn't mean you aren't good enough; it means the other person failed to notice what you had to offer.

Attributed to Mark Amend

I feel this is the kind of affirmation we need to say to ourselves and others again and again: if someone doesn't see your value, you really don't need them! If that person can't see the great things about you, they either haven't noticed or they're not looking properly. Either way, that's not what you need in your life. Don't let it stop you from knowing what you have to offer.

19 May

We're products of our past but we don't have to be prisoners of it.

Rick Warren

I once had a counsellor who said to me, 'Trauma is inevitable but it doesn't have to be a life sentence.' I've thought a lot about that since and the more I think about it, the truer it feels. Ultimately, though, nothing external is going to set you free; it's your mindset or making the brave decision to put your trust in something bigger than you entirely.

20 May

Tell the negative committee that meets inside your head to sit down and shut up.

Ann Bradford

When I first read this affirmation, it made me laugh out loud! I had never thought of the negative voices in my head as a committee, but it can feel like that sometimes. It's quite right, we do need to be firm with ourselves. We need to silence those doubting, unhelpful voices and allow space for more positive thoughts and feelings in our heads! What negativity can you tell to sit down and shut up today?

21 May

One loyal friend is worth more than a thousand fake ones.

I'm pretty sure social media has trained us to think that the most popular people are the ones with the largest numbers of 'friends', but, in fact, very few of those 'friendships' will have any real depth or add any value to the person's life. Rather than worrying about accumulating 'friends', I've found that it's more important to invest in and cultivate a few really amazing friendships.

I will stop waiting for things to happen and make them happen.

Often I find that people think opportunity will come and smack them in the face. Actually, it rarely presents itself in an obvious way. When you expect things to just turn up, you can start to resent those who achieve and see them as 'lucky'. The truth of it is that a lot of blood, sweat and tears has probably gone into getting them where they are. Do you need to stop expecting things to just happen? Where could you seek out opportunity today?

I have told you these things, so that in me you may have peace. In this world you will have trouble. But take heart! I have overcome the world.

John 16.33

There is something so much bigger than our current problems. For me, that perspective is really important. Often, I can have a horrible feeling in my stomach and have to think through what the source of the stress is, but when I identify it, I try to acknowledge that trouble will come and then I will welcome a sense of peace. It makes all the difference.

Everything will be OK in the end; if it's not OK it's not the end.

Attributed to John Lennon

I know this affirmation is a bit of a well-known one, but I still take comfort in it! When I'm in the middle of something, I always draw on this and say to myself, 'There's more to this – I just don't see it yet.' Is there a situation about which you can draw comfort from the idea that it doesn't feel right because it's just not over yet?

25 May

Don't waste your energy trying to change opinions . . . Do your thing and don't care if they like it.

Tina Fey

(*Bossypants*, Sphere, 2012)

Someone once said to me that there are people out there who have formed opinions about you based on virtually nothing. It could be from a one-minute interaction or the opinion of someone else. What are we going to do about that? Track down everyone who's ever heard of us to make sure that all their facts are correct and their opinion of us is good? No way! The fact is, we can't change how people perceive us, so let's save our energy and stop focusing on it!

26 May

No one can make you feel inferior without your consent.

Eleanor Roosevelt

(*Reader's Digest*, September 1940, Vol. 37, p. 84)

When it comes to other people's words, we can't control what they say, but we can control what we accept. It is hard to stop things having an impact, but if you can be robust and stick to what you know to be true, it makes all the difference. What is most important is what *you* think of *yourself* and how proud you are of your own actions, not what someone else says.

I will recognize and embrace all of the emotions that I was designed to feel.

It's important to allow yourself to experience your feelings. It can sometimes feel as if today's culture is rife with toxic positivity, and the need to put a positive spin on whatever we are going through, but our emotions are a positive thing and we shouldn't be afraid to feel them. Tears can be a physical release of built-up tension. Don't suppress the force of your emotions. Take some time out and allow yourself to feel them.

28 May

Love looks through a telescope and envy looks through a microscope.

Josh Billings

I really relate to this analogy. I've found that love is so broad and looks far and wide, so those who think through the lens of love are often broad-minded. In my experience, those who, instead, are caught up in envy can really have their blinkers on. Sometimes they can be selfish or nit-picking as a result. Love changes the people we show it to but, in the process, it changes us. Who could you show some love to today?

I can be brave, just like others I see.

When you see someone who has been brave, whether in the media or in person, it's important to remember that they don't have a superpower. They've been brave because, in that moment, it was their only choice. Often people have been presented with a difficult situation and, in order to carry on, they had to have courage. That same courage is in all of us. What situation would benefit from your bravery today?

Releasing shame changes the game.

I think the nastiest places on the Internet (and, therefore, probably in the world) are the comments sections and forums where people jump in and try to shame others. I've given up reading comments, for my own sanity. I wish we could all focus on spreading love and encouragement instead of anonymous hate from behind an avatar. When I stopped following and caring about these shaming comments, it really was a game changer for me.

31 May

I will find a place of refuge.

I never thought that I would end up going to church – I didn't think they'd want me! When I was younger, I was a total wild child – drinking, smoking and partying. I was so worried that I wouldn't be welcome because I hadn't lived a 'perfect life', I played down my past and tried to minimize it. Then I met people from so many different walks of life – a former heroin addict, someone who had run away from home and gone into care and all kinds of other people with different histories. Church as a safe space became really important to me. Where can you feel safe to be yourself, warts and all? Maybe it's a friend's house or in a support group or with your family or in a church. Whatever that looks like for you, we all need a place to feel safe.

June

1 June

I won't let a bad day become a bad week, month or year.

We all have bad days, when things don't go our way and we're disappointed by the outcome. I've found that it's so important not to allow those disappointments to spill over into other aspects of my life and ruin not only that moment but also that day, week or month. I try to stop negative incidents taking more space in my life than they need to.

June

2 June

If someone acts out because you set boundaries, it's simply more evidence that the boundary is needed.

It's not cruel to set boundaries, even if it feels like it at times. Being clear about your capacity within a relationship is the kindest thing that you can do. If someone can't respect your boundaries, then they're probably thinking more of their needs than of yours. Sometimes it's just where that person is at right now and it's a short-term thing, but if you find a friend consistently not respecting your requests, it might be time to have a conversation with them.

3 June

I have permission to think that I am good enough.

Sometimes it's more comfortable to put ourselves down than risk looking big-headed. I know a lot of women find it easier to point out their flaws than to highlight their great attributes, but I think that low self-esteem has to be challenged! It's not showing off or self-promoting to say, 'You know what? I am good enough.' You can and should be your biggest cheerleader!

4 June

Shame corrodes the very part of us that believes we're capable of change.

Brené Brown

(*I Thought It Was Just Me*, JP Tarcher/Penguin Unam, 2008)

If there's something in your life that you feel you're doing wrong or something in your past that you feel you shouldn't have done, then it's right to identify it and take steps to change and grow so you don't continue along the wrong path. I've found that shame can become so crippling, it prevents positive change from happening. As researcher and author Brené Brown shows us in today's affirmation, we need to stop dwelling in our shame and know that we can do better!

5 June

So do not fear, for I am with you;
do not be dismayed, for I am
your God. I will strengthen you and
help you; I will uphold you with my
righteous right hand.

Isaiah 41.10

Fear can cause so much damage in our lives. I don't know
about you, but I've found that simply telling myself to stop being
afraid doesn't work at all. Instead, I focus on the promise that
I am looked after and loved and, in that light, the world looks
less scary. How can you choose faith over fear today?

6 June

Do an act of kindness: message someone to tell them how well they're doing.

I love the idea that we can all be sending these little encouraging messages to each other and not expect anything in return. How often do you get that in life these days?! To receive an unprompted message telling you that you're smashing it – when you may feel you're doing anything but – is really special. So, who are you messsaging today?

7 June

The more grateful I am, the more beauty I see.

Mary Davis

(*Every Day Spirit*, Rich River Publishing, 2019)

I've always felt that it is my choice to see things a certain way. When I choose to be in a place of thankfulness for the things around me, everything feels that little bit better. I think of gratitude as the wine of the soul and, unlike alcohol, there's no such thing as too much – go ahead and get drunk on gratitude! You can never be too grateful.

8 June

Disappointment is just the action of your brain adjusting itself to reality after discovering things weren't the way you thought they were.

Brad Warner

(*Zen Wrapped in Karma Dipped in Chocolate*, New World Library, 2010)

Ultimately, if we can adapt, we can survive disappointment. Being adaptable is so important in a changing world. I know, when I was younger, I had such set ways I wanted things to go in my life – in reality, none of that stuff ended up happening! I don't regret the way my life has turned out at all, though. I just had to adapt to what was handed to me.

You are not your mistakes; they are what you did, not who you are.

Lisa Lieberman-Wang

I truly believe in rehabilitation, and thank Lisa very much for giving me permission to quote her wise words here. I believe everyone should have the chance to do things better next time. From the small mishaps all the way to those people coming out of prison, I hate the idea of condemning someone or writing them off as a lost cause when, really, who you are and your mistakes are two different things. We've all done things in the past that we don't associate with who we are now and we all need another chance.

10 June

I will let go of the life I expected to have and start living the life I was given.

At some point, you've just got to give in and accept where you are. I know, for me, my twenties didn't turn out how I planned them at all. My life was flipped completely upside down, but the longer I resisted that fact, the slower my recovery was. The moment I practised acceptance was the moment things changed. It freed up my headspace to focus on getting better and made life so much easier.

11 June

The trick, my brethren and sisters, is to enjoy the journey, traveling hand in hand, in sunshine and storm, as companions who love one another.

Gordon B. Hinckley

(*My Dear Sisters: Inspiration for Women*, Covenant Communications, 2008)

Community has been so important to me. Ultimately, we can look at difficult situations and feel defeated. In times like that, it's my faith and the loved ones around me that gets me through. It gives me the strength and encouragement to keep going. I believe that we can all achieve so much with a little help from our friends and a little bit of faith.

12 June

Let's not allow ourselves to be upset by small things we should despise and forget. Remember 'Life is too short to be little'.

Dale Carnegie

(*How to Stop Worrying and Start Living*, Cedar, 1993)

It's so easy to spend time obsessing over what people will say about you and what they will think of your choices. In the end, no matter what you do, the way people perceive you is completely out of your control, so I don't even bother trying to pander to it. What's more important to me is to focus on my own priorities and goals and not let what other people say play a part in my decision-making process.

13 June

Feeling gratitude and not expressing it is like wrapping a present and not giving it.

William Arthur Ward

Gratitude can be so moving that we often feel we have to communicate it to the person who sparked it. There are times, though, when something stops us. We can worry that people will think we're being silly or overly emotional in expressing our heartfelt thanks, but we need to. If we don't, it's like caring for somebody and never telling them. I always think that gratitude is there to be shared. Is it really gratitude if you never express it?

Someone is sitting in the shade today because someone planted a tree a very long time ago.

Warren Buffett

(<www.forbes.com> Warren Buffet Best Quotes)

The thought of this warms my soul. How lovely is the idea of laying down roots now to help others in the future! We benefit so much from the hard work of people who came before us, like the people who fought for civil rights or for women's right to vote. Our actions have a longevity that we may not even realize. How can you plant a seed now that will benefit future generations? Maybe it's by doing something to look after the environment or donating money to a research charity. Every small action counts.

15 June

Social media has created jealous behaviour over illusions. Sadly, some are jealous of things, relationships and lifestyles that don't even exist.

I've found a big problem with the way people approach social media is that they don't realize it's an advertising platform. It's like when you're watching TV and you have to sit through the ad break, but on social media it can be snuck in so it's not always clear what's real and what's designed by an advertising team. You don't need to berate yourself. You're definitely not inadequate if you don't match up to those pictures. They are all designed by professionals to look like something you're not, in the hope that you'll buy something they say will get you there. It's not bad to sell things online, but everyone should be aware that they're being sold to.

**I remain confident of this:
I will see the goodness of the LORD
in the land of the living.
Wait for the LORD;
be strong and take heart
and wait for the LORD.**

Psalm 27.13 – 14

I know it doesn't feel like it sometimes, but goodness is all around us. When I don't feel I can see the goodness, I know it's important to take heart and be strong. Waiting for things to shift is hard but, for me, being able to rely on my faith for comfort helps me through those times when I feel like giving up.

It is in the darkest skies that stars are best seen.

Richard Paul Evans

(*Timepiece*, Pocket Books, 1997)

It's when the toughest times have hit in my life, or during my darkest nights, that I've found my greatest strength. They've also helped me to see the people I can truly rely on more clearly. It's those bright stars – the people, my passions – that help me get through. If you're suffering it's horrific, but maybe in the future you'll see a new meaning in that terrible time. Where can you see glimmers of brightness breaking through your dark night?

18 June

Be grateful when things are going your way; be graceful when they're not.

When things are going great in our lives, we graciously practise gratitude and we allow ourselves to feel it as a privilege. When they're not going so well, though, I've found it's very important to practise dignity. I say 'practise' because it is a skill that we all need to practise and it doesn't come easy! How could you practise grace for yourself and for others today?

Don't settle for a normal life. Not when you can enjoy the wonderful weirdness of being who God created you to be.

Craig Groeschel

(*Weird*, Zondervan, 2012)

In recent years I've realized that choosing to be 'normal' is, in itself, a restriction! Being normal means deciding what you think is ordinary and what people will like most, then trying to conform to it. But doing that means you're not allowing yourself to grow and you'll never learn who you really are. I don't know about you, but it's the 'abnormal' things about people that I often love the most!

My feelings and thoughts are valid.

Positive thinking and affirmations can sometimes make people feel that others are shutting them down. People sometimes ask me how to be happy all the time, and my answer is that we don't have to be! It's awful when you go to someone with your pain and they don't acknowledge it or they aren't listening properly. Sometimes you just want people to say that what you are going through sounds really hard. Such validation is powerful and, if no one else has said it to you today, the way you feel is valid and you don't have to feel bad about it!

Walls keep everybody out. Boundaries teach people where the door is.

Mark Groves

(Twitter @CreateTheLove, 5 February 2020)

I've found it is so important to remember that boundaries aren't shutting someone out; they're just keeping the relationship in its rightful place. That, ultimately, allows it to grow in a really healthy way. When I let someone take over all my time and headspace, the relationship (whether romantic, friendship, work or other) can become toxic and, eventually, it all turns sour. These days, I'm realistic about my time and capacity, and my relationships are far more fruitful as a result!

22 June

Being brave isn't the absence of fear. Being brave is having the fear and finding a way through it.

Bear Grylls

(Twitter, 20 August 2015)

I think we can see brave people around us, in life or in the media, and assume that they're fearless. I know I've done some pretty brave things, but I am definitely not free from fear. I've just learnt through experience and circumstance not to let that fear overcome me or stop me from moving forwards. Where's your fear today? How could you move through it?

23 June

Faith is unseen but felt, faith is strength when we feel we have none, faith is hope when all seems lost.

Catherine Pulsifer

(<www.stresslesscountry.com>)

I know that problems can pile up and feel like a total mountain you'll never be able to overcome, but never let yourself believe that you are hopeless. When I have something difficult to tackle, it's the faith I feel inside that keeps me going. I trust that my strength will grow, and I have hope that there will be a solution. What could you put a little bit of faith in today?

24 June

Character cannot be developed in ease and quiet. Only through experience of trial and suffering can the soul be strengthened, ambition inspired and success achieved.

Helen Keller

It's so true that the skills we develop in times of trial can really shape us. The more I think about so-called 'problems', the more I think that we should rename them! Are they 'problems' if they are helping us to grow in such amazing ways? It's through them that we develop into the people we're supposed to be.

25 June

Do an act of kindness: write a thank you note to the person who delivers your post or comes to take your rubbish away, or another unsung hero who helps you regularly!

Where I am in the UK, we are so privileged to have people delivering these services to us, but because they often come round when we're still asleep or out at work, we can just take them for granted. You don't have to wait till Christmas to show your appreciation. You can help to make them feel valued and respected by thanking them now!

26 June

I will listen and not interrupt.

Listening sounds like the easiest thing in the world. It involves just sitting there and not saying anything, doesn't it? In reality, it's not that at all! Listening isn't passive; it's an active thing and it's really hard work. It's tough not to interrupt or give your opinion, particularly when you disagree, but sometimes the best gift you can offer someone is a listening ear.

Trade your expectation for appreciation and the world changes for you.

Tony Robbins

(YouTube channel 'TonyTalk')

Feeling disappointment is a fact of life. Ideally, we'd all like to minimize it. What I've found is that you can't control how other people around you behave and, often, you can't control the outcome of a situation, but you can control your expectations going in. If you can stop yourself from building them up too high in the first place, you won't experience the same level of disappointment.

28 June

Breathing in, I calm body and mind. Breathing out, I smile. Dwelling in the present moment, I know this is the only moment.

Thich Nhat Hanh
(*Being Peace*, Parallax Press, 2020)

As a society, I feel we're all obsessed with living in the past or in the future; we're always reminiscing or on the move to somewhere else. It's very difficult for us to actually live in and fully experience the present. I know that I can find it really hard to do, but when I manage to let go of worry and just take in my surroundings, it's an incredibly freeing and fulfilling experience.

The lowly he sets on high, and those who mourn are lifted to safety.

Job 5.11

It's a real comfort to me that the Bible is full of references to the lost, the last and the least. We all have our times of mourning and grief and I think, in those moments, it's important to know you're being thought of. Could you use this as inspiration to reach out to someone who is mourning today?

30 June

I can stay positive when others are negative.

This is definitely an affirmation that you have to vocalize! I have to say this out loud repeatedly until I actually start to believe it. When people around you are down, fighting the urge to join them isn't easy. I have to tell myself not to get sucked in. We don't have to follow the crowd!

July

1 July

I will believe in myself.

I remember when I first started doing interviews years ago, a lot of journalists would ask questions about whether I was going to work now and if I thought that I would ever find someone to marry. My answer was, 'Of course I'm going to work. Of course I'm going to get married. I will be an asset to any relationship!' I didn't let their negativity rub off on me. I believed in myself. How can you believe in yourself and your value today?

2 July

I'm very picky with whom I give my energy to. I prefer to reserve my time, intensity and spirit exclusively to those who reflect sincerity.

Dau Voire

I've found that sincerity is such a valuable trait in those around me. Friends who just perform and pretend are hard to truly know and, therefore, truly love. Our energy is precious, so why waste it on people who can't return our attention with vulnerability and authenticity? Where will your time be best spent today?

3 July

I won't let fear of the future stop me from moving forwards.

We never know what's in the future, but we can't let that stop us from moving forwards. Sometimes all you can see is the next right step and choosing to move on to it feels like jumping into the unknown. For me, I call on my faith to help me make that move. Ultimately, I can't control the future, but it doesn't stop me from wanting to move forwards into it.

4 July

What if we said, 'She's beautiful but so am I,' instead of, 'She's beautiful and how do I measure up to her?'?

Someone once said to me that a candle doesn't get any darker if we light another candle. There is space for all of us to be beautiful, so one person shining brightly doesn't mean that you can't. I love the idea of us all recognizing and celebrating each other's strengths. Just think how much more we can achieve together when we build each other up rather than waste time comparing ourselves.

I won't be suspicious of kindness.

Sometimes someone will do something really nice for me out of the blue. It could be as small as holding a door open for me or giving me their seat on the Tube. I don't know about you, but when people are kind for no reason, I sometimes ask myself, 'Why are they doing that?', 'What do they want?' What I've learnt is there actually are people who are that kind! When I stop being suspicious, that thought is so comforting. In fact, we can all be kind people today!

6 July

At first dreams seem impossible, then improbable, and eventually inevitable.

Christopher Reeve

(*Nothing Is Impossible*, Ballantine Books, 2004)

When I'm starting out on something new, it almost feels as if it won't actually happen. Sometimes I can feel self-doubt or as if I should be 'staying in my lane'. In my experience, though, and seeing this with others, once you get started, your capabilities are so obvious, every small achievement affirms that you may just be able to do this. Then, before you know it, you're living your dreams! What feels impossible to you today?

Anxiety does not come from thinking about the future but from wanting to control it.

Kahlil Gibran

I don't know about you, but I find this quite challenging, because it makes it clear that anxiety isn't coming from a place of wanting to think ahead and dream; it's actually about control. It's natural to feel you'd like to be in control but, in fact, so little is determined by our actions and so much is outside of them, it's not possible. Are there things that you feel anxious about but, really, you just want to control them?

And we know that in all things God works for the good of those who love him, who have been called according to his purpose.

Romans 8.28

It is such a reassurance to me that God is working for my good. When I feel that something I have been hoping and praying for isn't happening, having this reassurance means I don't feel too sad about it. Maybe it just means that particular thing wasn't what was best for me; that one closed door will lead to another open one which will be even better for me.

Be careful when you follow the masses; sometimes the 'm' is silent.

I love a cheeky affirmation to mix things up! We can all get swept up in the energy of a crowd without stopping to ask ourselves if we actually want to be there. It's easy to do but the consequences can be disastrous. We can avoid mob mentality, though, by taking a step back and a deep breath and each asking ourselves, 'Do I really want to be a part of this?'

Gratitude turns what we have into enough.

Knowing that you have a lot and feeling thankful for it will definitely make you feel rich – it does me at least! It gives me that mindset of abundance which is so key to a feeling of fulfilment and satisfaction in my life. I stop craving for more or chasing after things I don't have and am able to look around and just enjoy the things I have in each moment. What one thing are you most grateful for today?

I think a hero is an ordinary individual who finds the strength to persevere and endure in spite of overwhelming obstacles.

Christopher Reeve

(*Still Me*, Arrow Books, 1999)

Nowadays, with everyone sharing their best selves on social media, we can feel the pressure to live 'extraordinary' lives. But living an extraordinary life isn't about followers or fashion or accolades. Some of the most heroic people I've met are seemingly ordinary people putting one foot in front of the other in the face of adversity.

12 July

I am confident.

I've written a couple of books on confidence in the past and I remember the editor of one saying that I really needed to explore the idea of confidence and nail down exactly what it was. So, after some research, I found that confidence and resilience go hand in hand. When you feel resilient, you're confident that bad things can come and you'll be able to bounce back. When it comes to difficulties in my job or relationships, I feel confident that I will be able to cope because of my faith in God and myself. Are you tying your confidence to external factors or do you feel resilient enough to know that you will be OK no matter what comes?

I don't have to be cheerful all the time. I will not be afraid to show people my uncomfortable side.

We can't always feel our best, physically or mentally, but I've learnt that I don't need to put on a brave face for everyone. Don't be scared to show people who you really are, and how you really feel. You don't need to be constantly upbeat and happy. In fact, others may feel closer to you when they see how real and vulnerable you can be.

14 July

Do an act of kindness: offer someone a friendly smile today.

For this act of kindness, I was going to suggest smiling at a stranger in the street, but decided that could get us into all kinds of trouble! Maybe you could give a smile to the cashier as you pay for your coffee or groceries today? Perhaps you could smile at a parent at school drop-off time who looks as if they are having a bad day? When you look for places to spread some cheer, you'll find them!

One is loved because one is loved. No reason is needed for loving.

Paulo Coelho

(*The Alchemist*, HarperCollins, 1995)

I've always felt that envy is a symptom of a lack of appreciation of our own uniqueness and self-worth. Feeling jealous is something we all experience from time to time. The best thing is to acknowledge it and move on, wishing the other person success and good things. When the jealousy does take root, that's when the toxicity can be really damaging. Sometimes I think we need to stop and remember that we are loved simply because we are loved. Each of us has something to give that no one else has. Don't spend time wanting someone else's gift. Embrace your own!

July

16 July

I cheer for people . . . I was raised to believe there's enough sun for everybody.

Tracee Ellis Ross

I think that many of us, but perhaps particularly women, have been made to feel 'it's her or me'. There's a real feeling that we have to compete with one another, but do you know what? When women support women, it is powerful; when people support people, it's powerful. It creates more opportunity for all of us. There's definitely enough room for every single one of us to succeed, and it'll be much more fun if we're working together, rather than against each other, and championing one another.

I will not focus on the negative voices around me.

Sometimes your own self-doubt isn't the problem; it can be the responses of the people around you, who tell you that you can't do it or you're crazy. Sometimes they can tell you that if someone else has done something similar, you shouldn't bother or maybe even tell you you're not good enough. Often, I've found that this reaction is a projection of their own fears and lack of self-belief, nothing to do with you at all.

18 July

There is more to me than yesterday.

Living in the present tense is such a challenge, but it's important to keep in mind that focusing on what's been won't change anything in your future. You're better off acknowledging the past for what it was, learning lessons from it and moving on with your head held high. For me, it's the only way to break free from regrets.

19 July

It is better to take refuge in the LORD than to trust in humans.

Psalm 118.8

I've found it's important to acknowledge that we, as people, are not the biggest things. There is somebody out there who's greater than us and should be who you put your faith in, not people. Realizing that people will let you down is an important part of letting go.

20 July

I will be willing to be a beginner every single morning.

Meister Eckhart

It's OK to be new. Everyone had to begin somewhere, so you shouldn't feel embarrassed or upset when you have to start from scratch. What I think is most impressive is when people persevere. You won't be a beginner for ever and just imagine how great it will feel when, after some hard work, it clicks into place for you!

I have been assigned this mountain to show others that it can be moved.

When the weather warms up, I always feel a bit more capable and as though I have a renewed energy. I often find it easier to let things go in the summer months and can be a bit more carefree than at other times of the year. I've also noticed that with the warm weather comes a kinder approach from others. With all this positivity in the air, summer can bring with it a sense of relief. To me, it says, 'Yes, I can do this!' Is there anything you've been putting off tackling that you could take a look at now? Maybe this is the time to move the mountain!

22 July

I won't focus on being busy, but on being productive.

In society, I find that we glorify being busy too much. There aren't any prizes for rushing round like mad and running ourselves into the ground! Rather than being mindlessly busy, I try to prioritize my time and focus on the things, and especially the people, that mean the most to me. When I am working, I try to make sure that time is used productively so I can relax and enjoy it when I clock off.

'Thank you' is the best prayer that anyone could say.

Alice Walker

Even if this book were not about having 'a little bit of faith', I would still have wanted to include this affirmation. I think this speaks to everyone, no matter what you believe: saying thank you is such a universal thing. I don't think that you always have to say the words – you can show people you're grateful in the way you respond to them. How can you say thank you to someone today?

24 July

I won't beat myself up for taking my foot off the pedal.

Sometimes it's OK to coast. There are times when things can feel overwhelming and you don't feel able to take on new projects or be proactive or push things forwards. That's OK. Allow yourself the grace of taking a step back when you need to.

One reason we struggle with insecurity: we're comparing our behind the scenes to everyone else's highlight reel.

Steven Furtick

(Twitter, 10 May 2011)

Social media is a curated highlight reel. For some of the bigger names, they've even got managers and experts pulling it all together. If you don't look like that person or you're not living that lifestyle, it's probably because you don't have the same budget to employ people to make it look that way! The fun thing about life is that we're all in it together. We're *all* perfectly imperfect – even if some people would have you believe otherwise!

26 July

Even though I walk through the darkest valley, I will fear no evil, for you are with me; your rod and your staff, they comfort me.

Psalm 23.4

With many of the Christians I've met (and that's quite a few now that I'm presenting the BBC's *Songs of Praise*!), I've noticed a confidence in them as they go through their lives. It's almost as though they have a trust that makes them feel safe and protected. What makes you feel safe and protected in your life?

27 July

I won't let the fear of pain cause me to shy away from love.

In all relationships, whether professional, platonic, romantic or anything else, people will let you down, and you will feel pain at times. I often wish they'd taught me that at school, because if you are expecting life to be perfect, it's impossible to prepare yourself for pain. It's so important to know that just because something is painful doesn't mean you're doing it wrong. It means you are human. It means you are living. Importantly, it means you are growing.

28 July

I will say sorry when I'm wrong.

Apologies are powerful. I know that I can find it hard to say sorry when I'm wrong, particularly with the people I'm closest to! Far from admitting weakness, saying sorry shows your huge strength. It takes humility to recognize your own part in a situation, back down and make amends. I've always thought that people who apologize well show great character. Could you be that person today?

29 July

Often disappointment simply redirects you to the place you are meant to be.

Let-downs in life can be the catalyst for change. Sometimes, the change is unwelcome, which will push you out of your comfort zone, but that's when you can start to make new discoveries about your character. I am finding, as I get older, I can take such trials better than I used to because I can anticipate that although it might not feel right for me at the time, it might lead to something better.

When love is real, whether it's ebbing or flowing, it's always there, it never goes away.

Aidan Chambers

(*This Is All*, Bodley Head, 2005)

We can all go through phases when we aren't very lovable, when times get hard or things are stressful. I know that there are moments when I don't feel lovable at all! It's at those times that our friendships are more valuable than ever. I always feel that if friends stick around and show me the same support during times of hardship as they do in times of success, I can be confident in the strength of those relationships – that the love is real, as Aidan Chambers says. Who can you show love to today, even if they're going through a 'not-so-lovable' phase?

F-E-A-R has two meanings: 'Forget Everything And Run' or 'Face Everything And Rise'.

Zig Ziglar

There are two different approaches when it comes to fear. I don't know if it's the same for you, but I've tried both in my time! Ultimately, though, in recent years my mindset has changed; I feel far readier now to face up to the things I'm afraid of than I did, and the result of doing so has always been a boost for me.

What scary thing in your life could you face up to today?

August

1 August

Surround yourself with people who are willing to elevate and celebrate you.

It's our personal responsibility to make sure we surround ourselves with positive things. That includes the people in our lives and the people in our social media feeds. We always talk about social media as if it's this horrible beast, but there's so much good in it too. It's given a voice to the voiceless and I love using my own social media to provide a platform for things that matter. So, you just need to decide which positive voices you want to welcome on to your feed today.

2 August

Do an act of kindness: donate to charity or, if you don't have the money right now, share about their work on social media.

Charities often take on the really tough jobs, looking after the people or issues in desperate need of attention. I know from running a charity myself how tight the funding can be and how much we rely on the donations of others. If you don't have the cash right now, it doesn't mean that you are unable to do your bit. You could pick a charity that does great work and shine a light on it on social media today. The more publicity they get the better, and maybe someone you're connected with will decide to get behind them with a cash donation after reading your post!

I will stop trying to find my joy in all the wrong places.

When I look back at my younger years of partying, I realize that I was quite troubled and searching for something greater than myself. I always felt alone and looked for highs and fulfilment and protection in the wrong things and people. When I found my faith, I also found a comfort that I didn't experience in all that empty searching and it has meant so much to me.

Is there a gap in your life that you're trying to fill with the 'wrong things'? Is there something healthier you could turn your attentions to?

4 August

When it comes to life the critical thing is whether you take things for granted or take them with gratitude.

G. K. Chesterton

When I think about the people I've met who are the most fulfilled and enriched, I've found they're rarely those who have the most material things. Instead of accumulating stuff, they just feel grateful for the things they have. I understand, as I feel so grateful to have sight in one of my eyes. I could very easily be blind, so I feel thankful every day for that eye. I have less than someone with two good eyes, but I probably appreciate my sight more than they do. Perspective is life-changing.

What could you be more grateful for?

Every new beginning is an old new beginning's ending.

All things are so intertwined but, rather than feeling held back by that, I find it liberating! It's the circle of life. There's no need to get down about the endings, because they signal new beginnings. It's also important to remember that each new beginning will end at some point. I find great peace in accepting that idea.

6 August

I will not allow myself to be held back.

I've noticed a pattern among my girlfriends (and previously myself) that whenever someone goes through a break-up, they get out there and try new things or maybe change their hair or their job. Part of that, I'm sure, is trying to establish something that's just theirs, away from the person they've broken up with. I wonder if another part of it is them suddenly feeling freer – perhaps their partner was, consciously or unconsciously, holding them back. Is there anything that could be holding you back from making a positive change?

I will breathe.

We hear about this all the time today, and it took me a while to jump on the deep-breathing bandwagon, but I now find meditation to be such a valuable tool. Simply taking time to breathe in and out slowly gives me a sense of calm. When things get a bit much today, could you spare a moment to take a deep breath in and out? Better yet, could you try to find five minutes of quiet to focus on your breathing?

8 August

Sometimes good things fall apart so better things can fall together.

Attributed to Marilyn Monroe

I love the idea of handing over control of the things in my life to someone or something bigger than me. Just like this affirmation from actress and icon Marilyn Monroe says, I lean on my faith when things fall apart and trust that something better will fall together. Also, believing that means I don't have to take control on my own, which is really freeing. I can just trust and let go of the outcome!

For the Spirit God gave us does not make us timid, but gives us power, love and self-discipline.

2 Timothy 1.7

When I made the decision to start on my journey of faith, I noticed some changes pretty quickly. I found myself feeling more robust, more capable, more able, as well as softer and less angry. Those changes were so key for my development and helped me to become the person I am today. How do you see yourself growing in the coming months? How would you like to?

10 August

Do something today that you'll feel thankful for tomorrow.

Sometimes the last thing you want to do is look after yourself, but doing so today is the best investment in your future. I try to exercise regularly, but there are days when I really don't want to. I always try to push through that feeling, though, because I know my future self (even me in one hour's time!) will be grateful.

11 August

I will recognize that if someone treats me badly, it says more about them than it does about me.

We say to children all the time that if they're getting picked on in the playground, the bully has issues to work through and it's actually not about the child on the receiving end at all. Sadly, I find the same often translates into adult life. A person may be out and out rude to you or subtly putting you down with doubts and naysaying. I've found it so key in such situations to know that they're the one with the issue, not me.

12 August

Small acts, when multiplied by millions of people, can transform the world.

Howard Zinn

(*A Power Governments Cannot Suppress*, City Lights, 2006)

The power of a group of people rising up in support of a common cause is phenomenal, but when you break up that group, it consists of little parts. I know I can sometimes feel that there's no point trying to change society, as if I'm banging my head against a brick wall and my little vote won't make a difference, but that couldn't be more wrong. If all of us did nothing, nothing would be done. Each of us has something valuable to offer, and if we were to all realize that, just imagine the difference we could make!

13 August

I will choose community over competition.

Over the years I've found that doing things in community with others is often the best way forward. My experience has shown me that it's a far more contented and fulfilled path than each person selfishly pursuing their own gains. You'll find that your progress will be limited if you go it alone anyway. The fact is, we can get much further and achieve much more as a group.

What could you invite other people into today?

14 August

I will believe in things that I cannot see.

Sometimes people ask me about my faith and say, 'How can you believe in God? You've never seen him.' The fact that I can't see him is what creates the faith. I came to the idea of God with an open heart and found so much beauty in it. Is there something you've dismissed that you could explore again with an open heart?

The best feeling ever is realizing that you aren't sad any more about something you were sure you'd never get over.

I love the feeling you get when you've moved past something that used to cause you huge pain. For me, when I look back at things I thought I'd never get over and realize that I have, I feel a kind of euphoria! Next time you're in a place where something is upsetting you and ruling your thoughts, just remember how it feels to move past it and hang on to that promise. There will be a time when you'll look back and that feeling of pain will be just a memory and the euphoria of getting through it will be yours.

16 August

The only problem we really have is we think we're not supposed to have problems! Problems call us to a higher level – face and solve them now.

Tony Robbins

(Twitter, 25 October 2013)

When I was younger, I always felt terrified of having to face any dark times. That didn't stop them coming, but what comes out of them, I've often found, is that I'm pushed to elevate myself to the next level. It's the reason, I believe, that so many famous faces and big names in business have memoirs that tell of their pain and trials. I don't think it's a coincidence that they've had to work through hard things and now are really successful! Is there a problem that could be an opportunity in your life?

I will celebrate everyday wins, big or small.

I've found that it's so important to celebrate the little wins in each day. I like to go wild for the big things too but, of course, they're fewer and further between. I congratulate myself for getting up without snoozing my alarm or doing some exercise even when I didn't feel like it! Marking these small milestones gives me appreciation for the progress I am making. What were your small wins today?

Setting goals is the first step in turning the invisible into the visible.

Tony Robbins
(<www.tonyrobbins.com/tony-robbins-quotes>)

Sometimes, it's good to get practical. If there's something I'm working towards, I start with goal-setting and break the task down into more manageable chunks. I know sometimes people can feel embarrassed to write down or talk about their goals, because they're worried people will think they're silly, but it's great to work towards something you care about. Don't ever feel ashamed of doing it!

What is taken for granted eventually will be taken away.

I'm big on self-care and speaking kindly to myself, but also, sometimes, I need a bit of tough love! For me, this affirmation is more about our treatment of others than the material possessions we have. If you take a person in your life for granted, whether that's a personal or professional relationship, that person will get fed up and may eventually give up on your relationship if you don't change. Who could you show your appreciation for today? Could you drop them a message now?

20 August

For we are God's handiwork, created in Christ Jesus to do good works, which God prepared in advance for us to do.

Ephesians 2.10

This idea of there being works that have been prepared in advance for us to do is really interesting. To my mind, it comes down to purpose. There were times with the charity when I needed to do a big funding drive to be able to pay for something. I've never had any training in fundraising, so it didn't come naturally, but the right people cropped up to guide me through it and it became easy enough in time. Seeing it as my purpose meant that I felt confident to push through and develop the skills I needed to do it.

Do an act of kindness: introduce yourself to a neighbour you don't know.

During the pandemic, particularly when we all had to stay at home, many of us connected much more than usual with our neighbours, which was a real silver lining to a dark cloud. All I could think was, 'Why didn't I do this sooner?' If there's someone who's recently moved in or you've never connected with, why not knock on the door and say hi? You never know, it could be the start of something great!

22 August

I will not let my worry control me.

There's no reason for your problems to get the better of you. Keeping your mind in a place of positivity and affirming yourself will help you to believe that. Hopefully, using this book is a good first step in that direction! The fact is, we are always bigger than our problems, so they don't need to overwhelm us. Stand up tall and say it out loud again: 'I will not let my worry control me.' How did that feel?

23 August

Compare yourself only with yourself. You don't know others' full story.

Doe Zantamata

(Karma CreateSpace Independent Publishing Platform, 7 February 2012)

When we begin to dream about a change in our lives, or a new project or passion, it's easy to compare ourselves to other people and discount ourselves as 'not as good as them' or 'not good enough' full stop. But it would be such a shame if you gave up on pursuing something that could be incredible because you were afraid of what could happen. When we start letting fear dictate our decisions and actions, we're letting it win. What could you take action with today, despite your fear?

24 August

I will remember that no one's life is perfect, even if it seems that way.

It's so easy to look at what someone else has and wish we had it for ourselves, but the reality is never what it seems. Of course, I don't want to picture all the terrible things that could be going on behind the scenes but, in my experience, it's important to remember that you don't know the full extent of someone else's situation. If, however, someone is as successful and happy as they appear, why not feel pleased for them? Troubles come for all of us so they should be allowed to celebrate this time of success!

25 August

I am, quite simply, amazing.

Sometimes the most straightforward statements are the most underrated. When was the last time you reminded yourself that you're amazing? Don't think that the only amazing people are the overachievers or the people on telly. You are amazing, for the way you support your loved ones and take each day as it comes!

26 August

Opportunities are everywhere — I just need to choose to see them.

We all have a friend who loves a good moan. On the wrong day, that friend could be me! I've found that attitude is really important. If you can, get into the mindset that nothing is set in stone and you can change things at any time — you will find you feel freer. Opportunity is everywhere, if you're open to seeing it.

For all have sinned and fall short of the glory of God.

Romans 3.23

I feel that most of us, religious or not, have built up this big, scary idea of a judgement day, when we'll find out who's been good and who's been bad. Actually, in a weird way, this verse is comforting — because we all do bad things. There isn't anybody who can reflect back and say that they've never done anything wrong. I don't know about you, but when I was younger, I would see certain people as perfect, like my teachers or people in authority or my parents. As I've grown up (and become a parent myself!), I know that we're all only human.

28 August

My past is not a weapon to be used against me.

I remember a news story about a person in the public eye who was being 'outed' by Internet trolls for having previously been a sex worker. The individual addressed the claims, confirmed them and apologized for any shame she had brought on her family or the people she worked with. In response, the outpouring of love from her colleagues and followers was so inspiring. In the end, something that could have been eating away at her as a 'shameful secret' for years probably gained her more respect and more fans than would have been the case if this had never happened. I found that story so inspiring. Never be afraid of your past!

What we call failure is not the falling down, but the staying down.

Mary Pickford

(*Sunshine and Shadow*, Doubleday, 1955)

In our culture, failure has such negative connotations. Society has framed failure as a bad thing, but if you were learning to play the piano, you would have to play a song hundreds of times before you could do it perfectly! Each of those attempts is a failure to play it perfectly, but is that bad? Of course not! It's a necessary part of getting it right.

30 August

In order to feel love, I will experience pain – and that's OK.

I wish, as children or young people, we were taught that pain is not only an acceptable but also a necessary part of love and relationships. Instead, we're all taught to avoid feeling hurt, sometimes at all costs, when it's actually unavoidable. I've learnt that just because something causes you pain, it doesn't mean you're doing it wrong or making the wrong decisions. You're just showing up and being vulnerable, and you should be very proud of that.

Worry doesn't empty tomorrow of its sorrow. It empties today of its strength.

Corrie Ten Boom

(*Clippings from My Notebook*, Triangle, 1983)

We all know that worrying is counterproductive, but I still do it! I therefore have to work really hard to remind myself that it doesn't add to the future, just detracts from the goodness in the present, and that helps me to refocus. Do you need to refocus today?

September

1 September

Autumn whispered to the wind, 'I fall; but always rise again.'

Angie Weiland-Crosby

There's so much power in the idea of rising again. This quote reminds me of the famous poem 'Still I rise', by author and activist Maya Angelou. It's the idea that you can get knocked down, or just fall down, but, no matter what, you will get up again, you will rise. This idea makes me feel empowered and excited at the same time.

2 September

I will never regret being kind.

I think the thing that holds a lot of people back from apologizing or showing someone an act of kindness is worry about how they'll respond, but it's not what they do in return that matters. If you know that you've behaved well, you can hold your head up high. You will never look back and say that you wish you were rude to that person, but you're definitely likely to regret it in the other direction. Kindness is an approach you can always trust.

If it doesn't challenge you, it won't change you.

Over the years, I've learnt to love and embrace a challenge. If someone asks me to do something new, I rarely confess that I don't know how. I run at it head on and try to work it out as I go. Sometimes it doesn't work, but that's how I evolve and grow. I challenge you to say yes to one new thing today.

4 September

There are far, far better things ahead than any we leave behind.

C. S. Lewis

(Letter to Mary Willis Shelburne, 17 June 1963, in C. S. Lewis, *Letters to an American Lady*, Wm. B. Eerdmans, [1963] 2014. © copyright UK CS Lewis Pte Ltd 1963; USA Wm. B. Eerdmans, [1963] 2014. Reprinted with permission.)

I know that everyone has a past. I also know that it's totally normal to reflect on your past. When I start to feel down about things that happened long ago, I find it's important to remember that whatever is in the future, it will be better and greater than before. In my life, I trust that what God has in store for me is what is right, and I won't regret it!

I will forgive myself.

Forgiving is difficult, but what's even harder than forgiving those around us is forgiving ourselves. Offering yourself understanding and grace is tough, and I know – I can be my own worst critic. Be kind to yourself, treat yourself with the same love and care that you would a friend. What do you need to forgive yourself for today?

September

6 September

We rise by lifting others.

Robert Ingersoll

Over the years, I've had the opportunity to help others —
sometimes financially, but often in other practical ways, like
with mentoring or opening the door to an opportunity for
someone. My motivation is never what I can get back but,
at times, completely unexpectedly, people have helped me
in incredible ways. My experience is that the good you offer
others always comes back around.

7 September

I will see the value in collaboration.

We may often feel we can't be bothered to get other people involved in our projects – or even our lives! I know I've felt that there's no point sometimes, because those people may let me down or hurt me. What I've learnt in the past few years, though, is that there really is strength in numbers and when you allow people into your project or vision and collaborate with them, it is powerful.

8 September

The secret of your success is determined by your daily agenda.

John C. Maxwell

(*Make Today Count*, FaithWords, 2008)

Absolutely everything good I've achieved in life has come from consistency. If you want to be successful in business or build great relationships or lose some weight, the trick is to do the same things over and over. Often we'll be told that all we need is to read this book or buy that gadget or take those miracle pills, but there are no quick fixes. As John Maxwell points out above in the subtitle of his book, it's our daily habits that build who we are and take us to where we want to be.

Do an act of kindness: help someone with their pushchair.

Trying to navigate the world with a pushchair, a baby and all the other bits you need to lug around to look after it is seriously tough – particularly if you've been up half the night! There are times when parents feel at breaking point. There's such a sense of relief as a new parent when someone stops to offer you a hand – it feels as if that person is an angel, sent just for you! Who could you lend a hand to today?

10 September

If you believe, you will receive what you ask for in prayer.

Matthew 21.22

I find it difficult when people try to dissect my faith. I've often been asked questions about why things happen as they do and why God doesn't seem to answer all our prayers. In my experience, it simply doesn't work like that. For me, it's about having faith and keeping that faith alive while putting in some of the practical work yourself. I've found that we have to be partners in the process – praying but also taking action and acknowledging that God doesn't always answer prayers in the time or in the way we had hoped.

I won't minimize the pain I feel.

I believe that pain has the ability to change the way people look at and respond to their everyday life. It can be so draining to constantly feel hurt by disappointments or difficult life circumstances. I've found that the only way to recover from such pain is to allow myself to feel it, without trying to numb it or pretend it's not there.

12 September

I will focus on the best elements of my day.

When I sit down at the end of the day to think about how it went, I always try to focus on the best parts. I know that we need to acknowledge the bad, but so often we *only* acknowledge the bad. We need to start telling ourselves a different story, to focus on the time spent with loved ones, the uplifting conversations and all those glorious small wins!

I won't chase other people's achievements.

If you constantly covet someone else's things or accomplishments or life, then you will always be dissatisfied with what you have. What happens when you finally reach that person's level? Often that's when you find out you've been on an unfulfilling quest and you then want what's next or what someone else has. Take some time to look back on the things you have achieved in the past few years – have you stopped celebrating them too soon?

14 September

I am not stupid if I get something wrong.

I feel so frustrated by people feeling stupid or, worse, being made to feel stupid for getting something wrong. I get things wrong all the time. We all do! It's how we learn. When I get something wrong, that's when I push myself to develop the most, so how can that be stupid?!

Even when I'm struggling, I'm moving forwards.

The idea of 'keeping calm and carrying on' can make me feel so frustrated when I'm in the middle of something! It's the struggles that we face, though, that do move us forwards. Being resilient isn't being immune to hurt; it's feeling hurt but not allowing it to keep you where you are. We build resilience by continuing to move forwards – not in massive leaps, but small, triumphant baby steps.

16 September

I will appreciate the past for what it was.

So long as we don't end up living in the past, sometimes it's positive to think about where we've been. That's partly because it shows us how far we've come and partly because we're allowed to feel fondness towards things that have been and gone. There are elements of my past that I wouldn't want back, but I can still appreciate them and the good times that I experienced.

17 September

I don't need to be in control.

If I feel stressed or anxious or out of control, I just try to surrender what I'm holding on to. For me, it's so freeing to relinquish control of my life and my problems to God and know that he will take over. It's tough to fight the urge to try to take charge, but there's so much freedom for me in trusting in a greater plan.

18 September

When we have each other, we have everything.

This affirmation was completely solidified for me during the COVID-19 pandemic and the subsequent lockdowns we had in the UK. I think those weeks and months taught us that, no matter what you have, if you don't have company or community, then you're not rich. Lots of people created new bonds with those in their homes, bubbles or communities, and those close relationships became really important. In the end, it's not what you do in life, it really is who you spend it with.

19 September

I will think of solutions.

I know this isn't always the right thing to say, and pushing ourselves to 'fix' things is sometimes damaging, but there are times when we're so focused on the problem that we don't see the solution. Other times, I think that the solution could be right in front of us but we don't see it because it doesn't look how we thought it would. Could you turn your attention to solutions today?

20 September

I will speak kindly and respectfully to myself.

There's a really good exercise someone once told me about that I use all the time. Picture your friend coming to you with a particular problem. Now write out what you would say to your friend. What would you write? It would be compassionate and kind, highlighting your friend's strengths. That's exactly how you should speak to yourself when you have a problem to tackle. Don't put yourself down, but treat yourself with the same love and compassion that you would give your friend. Seeing the words you would use written out is such a powerful exercise.

I won't worry about what could happen in the future. Instead, I will focus on what's happening in the present.

Someone once challenged me to look at all the things that have brought me the most fear and anxiety in my past. Then that person asked me to count how many of those things actually happened. What I realized is that the things we worry about most, often don't happen. Meanwhile, problems we never even imagined do crop up. Worrying doesn't prepare us for the future; it just takes us out of the present. Try to identify and let go of hypothetical worries today and focus on the now.

22 September

Bad experiences won't crowd my headspace.

As I write this, I am reminded that I had a difficult conversation about work yesterday. There were 24 hours that I lived through yesterday, though, and it didn't take up all that time — because I didn't let it. Despite that experience, I had real moments of joy and happiness and moments of feeling neutral yesterday as well. Is there anything that is stealing your peace today?

Rejoice always, pray continually, give thanks in all circumstances; for this is God's will for you in Christ Jesus.

1 Thessalonians 5.16–18

Loads of people who aren't religious pray every day because it's soothing and calming. Prayer is such a personal process but, for me, it can happen during meditation, while preparing a great meal to share or in talking to God while I'm out on a run. There's no right way to do it; just do whatever brings you the most peace and comfort.

24 September

Living with anxiety is like being followed by a voice, but I won't let it drown me out.

The voice of anxiety knows all our insecurities and uses them against us. It sometimes gets to the point where it's the loudest voice in the room, the only one you can hear. I'm not sure about you, but this description feels really relatable to me. It makes anxiety sound like a nit or something that lives in your hair but isn't actually a part of you. We will all experience some anxiety from time to time, that's normal. It's when the anxiety becomes louder and drowns out your own voice that it becomes a problem.

25 September

Conditions are never perfect. 'Someday' is a disease that will take your dreams to the grave with you.

Tim Ferriss

(*The 4-Hour Workweek*, Harmony, 2009)

I've stopped waiting for everything to fall into place before I try to achieve something. That's because I've realized that things are never perfect and I can never feel completely ready for anything, so why not just go for it now! I know a lot of people will feel that they should wait for 'A' before they go for 'B', but time will just keep passing them by. The fact is, 'someday' doesn't exist for anybody. Don't let life keep rolling on with you always saying, 'I'll do it tomorrow.'

26 September

A family doesn't have to be perfect, it just has to be united.

All relationships are complicated. People aren't perfect — I know I'm not! So forgiveness is key, because we will all make mistakes in life. Maintaining unity, even when someone has upset you, is a way of showing that person you have their back, no matter what, and we all need that.

I will not take a 'no' as a personal attack.

Any time I receive some form of rejection, I ask myself what the 'no' could mean. It could mean the timing's wrong, that the other person isn't ready for what I'm offering or already has something similar in the pipeline. A 'no' is rarely a reflection on you, so you shouldn't take it that way.

September

28 September

I will run my own race.

It's such a waste of time being jealous of those around you
– though when we're constantly bombarded with people's
highlight reels on social media, not comparing ourselves to
others can be easier said than done! The truth is, sometimes
you're ahead and sometimes you're behind, but the race is long
and, in the end, you're the only one who can run the perfectly
unique race designed for you. Is there someone you need to
stop comparing yourself to today?

Do an act of kindness: give something away to the charity shop today.

If you're anything like me, there will be clothes in your wardrobe that you haven't worn for a while. There's so much in the media at the moment about the lasting damage fast fashion is doing, so I'm really trying to do my best to get as much wear out of each item as I can. If there's something that I know I won't wear again, though, I give it away – either to a friend or to a charity shop – so that it can have a second life. Have you got some clothes you could give away? Someone else will be delighted to have found your top or dress and will get so much use out of it. You'll be doing your bit for the environment too!

30 September

I can handle whatever's thrown at me.

I heard someone say that God gives the toughest journeys to the strongest soldiers because they are the ones who can cope. You might agree that this seems to be the case in life generally. The more I think about it, the more it comforts me in hard times. I know that I can handle whatever is thrown at me, because I've got the strength and tools to do so.

October

Injustice anywhere is a threat to justice everywhere.

Martin Luther King Jr

Martin Luther King wrote those words in a letter from Birmingham Jail in April 1963, but we still need to work for unity and justice today. When I look around, it seems that we're becoming more and more divided and increasingly less tolerant of differing views. As a world, I think it's important to recognize that we should stand together against injustice. That is because when one person or group is being badly treated, it affects us all. Which person or cause could you stand up for today?

2 October

If you learn to really sit with loneliness and embrace it for the gift that it is . . . an opportunity to get to know YOU. . . you will realize that a little loneliness goes a LONG way in creating a richer, deeper, more vibrant and colorful YOU.

Mandy Hale

(*The Single Woman*, Thomas Nelson, 2013)

Sometimes we can get so caught up in the hustle and bustle of everyday life, in ticking off things on our to-do lists and rushing around, that we don't invest in ourselves. As difficult as quiet time can be, I've found it's when I'm on my own that I do my best thinking. Although I can find doing it very hard, I just have to remind myself to sit tight and feel what I feel, not stop it. Just because it's a period of difficult growth now doesn't mean that good things aren't coming in the future.

A relationship is a luxury in my life, not a necessity.

When I was single, I was so independent that when I met my husband, he was a luxury, not a necessity. I knew that I didn't need a guy to complete me – I was even looking into having a child by adoption or sperm donation, as I didn't have a partner. Taking responsibility for myself was empowering for me and helped me to appreciate a relationship when it came, but I didn't have to rely on it. Is there anything you're longing for that you feel is a necessity, but would actually be a luxury?

4 October

I can see the extraordinary in every ordinary person I meet – including myself.

My podcast is called *Extraordinary People* but, in reality, each person is an ordinary person who has something extraordinary inside. I've come to know that the 'extraordinary' can be found in absolutely anyone, if I tap into it. You may come across people who don't think that way, but that's shallow and sad for them because they will never see those incredible values and characteristics in a so-called 'ordinary person'. We are all extraordinary in our own way.

5 October

Being kind is giving even when it seems you have nothing to give.

Giving things away is an important part of living in community. It stops us from being self-centred and switches our focus away from ourselves. I don't always have the capacity to give my time and, when I was younger, I didn't have much money to give either! I have, though, always been able to give kindness. We all can. Kindness costs nothing but means everything.

6 October

Only a fool trips on what's behind him.

Monica Murphy

It's true that the past has its place. For starters, it shows us how far we've come. I can't believe how much I've grown over the past decade! Second, the past is a useful tool in directing our future decisions. Yet, we need to be careful not to be so focused on the past that it trips us up and keeps us there. Remember to keep moving forwards, towards your future – you'll be surprised all over again at how far you've come!

The LORD is close to the broken-hearted and saves those who are crushed in spirit.

Psalm 34.18

Sometimes we all need to feel someone close, especially when we feel low or broken-hearted. I find it so reassuring that God sees that and wants to comfort us in those times of pain. Is there someone in distress today whom you could hold close?

8 October

I will take the time to look for beauty today.

We can choose to step out of the door in the morning and keep our heads down or we can look up and see wonder all around us. Even through periods of lockdown or when our circumstances mean that we can't get out and about, the same applies; it's often not the scene that changes, it's our perspective. There is so much beauty in the people we see, the moments we enjoy and creation around us. Where can you see beauty today?

9 October

I will not play it safe.

Playing it safe seems like a good idea, but it offers people a false sense of security. Ultimately, everything we do involves a level of risk – even just popping to the shops for a loaf of bread or crossing the road or heading to work! We may as well take those risks, chasing things that we love and actually want. Even if something doesn't go how we'd like, at least we'll know that we tried.

10 October

Today, I will focus on one thing at a time.

Anyone who has gone through any kind of recovery that takes a long time will know this is key to that journey. There's no point projecting forwards. It helps us to keep going if we just focus on the day we are in and face the trials that come with it. Each day is substantial and really important.

Leave behind those who don't allow you to move forwards.

Often, we can be reluctant to stop seeing certain people because we're so desperate not to be rude! Obviously, it's important not to be rude to people, but we don't have to keep people in our lives at our own expense. It's important to surround yourself with positive people who champion you and encourage you to move forwards.

12 October

You do not find the happy life. You make it.

Attributed to Camilla Eyring Kimball

We all have to take personal responsibility for our lives and what we choose to make of them. In addition, I think it's important to remember that sometimes bad things happen at random and even if we plan our lives amazingly well, there will always be things that do not go as we'd hoped. That is why, even when you've put in the work to 'make' that happy life, be kind to yourself, manage your expectations and find happiness in the unexpected too.

13 October

I will learn to trust.

Putting our trust in something can make us feel really vulnerable because we leave ourselves open to being let down. Honestly, though, I have learnt how much better I feel when I trust in God. I realize that God doesn't always answer every prayer instantly and there's a lot of suffering in the world but, for me, trusting in God means letting go and feeling supported for the long run. That's a nice feeling of comfort for me, knowing that trusting can be the safest place of all.

14 October

Nothing is a failure; it's a rehearsal.

Life's too short to wonder 'What if . . . ?' I always throw myself into every project and give 100 per cent so that I never regret it when something doesn't work out. If that happens, I don't see it as failure; it was just me exhausting all options and working out what's for me and what isn't. What so-called failures in your life need to be reframed into fuel for the next part of your journey today?

15 October

I give myself permission to take a break.

I am a big fan of locking my office door for the weekend, partly so the kids don't get in and mess it up, but also so I won't be tempted to sneak in and work. It's a relief to turn the key in the lock and say to myself, 'Whatever hasn't been finished, I'm not going to let it seep into my weekend.' That boundary is important for me.

16 October

Sometimes I won't feel positive – and that's OK.

Sometimes I worry that the whole 'positivity movement' has ended up causing people damage. We can be so obsessed with 'staying positive' that we deprive ourselves of our natural emotions. Sometimes, I will even feel guilty about not feeling my best! If you're having a low day, know that you're allowed to feel that way, engage with your emotions and let it pass – you don't have to force yourself to be positive.

Do an act of kindness: bring the coffees to work unexpectedly for your co-workers.

People love a gift they aren't expecting and a nice coffee in the morning is just what some offices need to set them on a great footing for the day. Making your team's needs a priority will put people in a great mood and maybe it'll set off a chain reaction of kindness. Hopefully, because you've been kind to them, they'll be more inclined to show kindness in their next interaction and it could continue from there – like a Mexican wave of generosity!

October

18 October

I will just 'get on with it'.

When I was at my lowest point, my mum was quite funny. I remember crying to her one day and she simply said, 'Well, you're just going to have to get on with it, dear!' It's become a family in-joke that we say to each other when someone has a mountain to climb. It's not always a good idea to be so straight-talking with people, but sometimes bluntness is just what you need!

I sought the LORD and he answered me;
he delivered me from all my fears.

Psalm 34.4

This is the experience I had when I first had an encounter with God. I was at such a low place in my life, but when I surrendered, I felt so comforted. It meant that I got to hand over the burden of the things I was battling and I could trust I would be taken care of.

20 October

Comparing yourself to others is an act of violence against your authentic self.

Iyanla Vanzant

(Twitter, 3 September 2012)

I know that this is very heavy language and not a topic to be taken lightly, but the powerful imagery Iyanla Vanzant uses here is insightful. People can do things to physically hurt themselves, but they can cause themselves great mental damage too. Continually repeating bad things about yourself and allowing yourself to believe them will create deeper and deeper wounds. I think speaking in such brutal terms really drives home how important it is to be kind to ourselves. Don't dismiss the value of caring for yourself!

I won't place the value of my worth on the opinion of someone who fails to see it.

We've all put too much value on what others think of us, whether that's people we've dated or didn't end up dating, work colleagues or even individuals we don't know that well at all, but actually it's so irrelevant. When you build your life based on others' opinions, you end up feeling unfulfilled. What other positive, firm foundations can you build on today?

22 October

I don't know what's round the corner and I choose to let that excite me rather than scare me.

The mystery of what's coming next is both one of the best and one of the worst things about life. I choose to see the unknown as a place of opportunity and I am excited to see what's waiting for me. That can be a really tough attitude to take, though, particularly if you've experienced some real pain or trauma in your past. All the same, I like to allow myself to open up to the idea that better things are on the horizon and be excited about them!

If you don't know what your purpose is, let your passions lead the way.

I've often wondered if the constant search for purpose can become destructive when people don't find what they're looking for. It feels right to me that passion comes before purpose because, if we work out what fires us up the most, that's probably the area where we will be most motivated to work hard. Could you spend some time thinking about what you're most passionate about today?

24 October

I won't obsess about how things used to be.

I think we can all spend time longing for things in the past – I know that I've fallen into that trap! Before I became a mum, my lifestyle, my appearance and my body were so different, but I take comfort in knowing that nothing lasts and to live is to change. I've slowly learnt to appreciate the current moment I am in rather than long for what has been.

Time and pressure can turn coal into diamonds.

When I look back at my life experiences, I can see that, sometimes, it was the worst things that brought out my best character traits. If I hadn't struggled, I never would have known that I have resilience and courage. As someone who believes in and follows God, I know that he doesn't put us through difficult situations that we can't cope with but, rather, uses these for good, to help us to emerge from them as diamonds.

26 October

Kindness is the golden chain by which society is bound together.

Johann Wolfgang von Goethe

One act of kindness or a small gesture can start a ripple effect that has an impact on far more people than the one it was originally directed towards. I know I've seen that more than ever in lockdown during the pandemic. In 2020, I think we all witnessed small displays of kindness that carried through our communities. What kind act could you do to spread some love today?

I will respect myself by ensuring that others respect my boundaries.

I know that sometimes we can feel we owe people things – our time, our attention or our friendship. The problem is, this can lead us to sacrifice our own needs in favour of the needs of others. It's so important to establish boundaries and to enforce them. You won't be able to be a great friend to those around you if your mental health is suffering because you've taken on too much. Look after yourself first!

28 October

My life has more good than bad, even if it doesn't always feel that way.

There have been times when it has felt as though life is one long negative experience, with bursts of positive things happening now and then. What I know now is that, in fact, it's the opposite. I think that life is a rich experience with some difficulties throughout, and that's OK because the hardships don't last and good things can come from them too.

29 October

I haven't failed. I have learnt.

For me, the idea that 'nothing is a failure, just a rehearsal' is one that takes a while to sink in. I have to say it out loud over and over! The truth is, though, when we realize that our 'failures' help us to develop into the people we want to be and grow the skills we need, we will stop resenting them and embrace them.

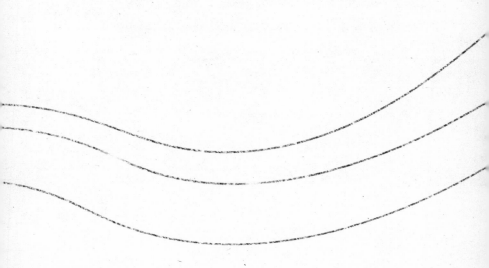

30 October

I will not live my life for other people.

It's so important to me that, at the end of my life, I won't look back and think, 'I lived my life for other people.' For me, as a Christian, caring for others is important and God makes it abundantly clear that he wants us all to love our neighbours. To live for their opinions or the opinions of anyone else other than him, however, is not what he wants, as it will always take us down the wrong path. Who are you living your life for today? Make sure you live for the thing that matters most.

Never apologize for saying what you feel. That's like saying sorry for being real.

Unknown

I think we can all agree that there are levels of honesty. If you don't like someone's outfit, you don't have to march over and tell them. That's basically trolling. If someone asks you your opinion, however, it's OK to be straight with them, in a kind way. We can get so caught up in people-pleasing that we apologize for our opinions and there's no need!

November

1 November

I won't be thrown off by changing circumstances.

It can be exhausting when the goalposts constantly shift. I know I felt that way during the COVID-19 pandemic when there were so many changes to what the restrictions were. It almost felt as if every time I got used to the new circumstances and told myself I could handle them, suddenly they all changed. I don't know what your experience has been, but I actually learnt a lot about myself in that time. Whenever there was a change, it forced me to dig a little deeper and draw on my strength and courage. Now that we have managed to get through the first and subsequent lockdowns, I truly believe that we can confidently face change, knowing that we are able to adapt!

2 November

Feel the fear and do it anyway.

Susan Jeffers

(*Feel the Fear and Do It Anyway*, Vermilion, 2007)

Bravery shouldn't be underestimated. It's not easy to force yourself to do something that scares you. Often, you'll find that thing less and less scary the more you do it. I remember when I first started doing public speaking, seeing all those faces looking back at me was terrifying! With time, I got used to it and I'm so proud of myself for persevering. What scary thing can you do today?

Shame, like beauty, is often in the eye of the beholder.

Julie Burchill

From time to time, I've confided in someone and found their response to be a little judgemental or maybe even disapproving, but I haven't felt embarrassed by the situation; it's just a part of who I am. It's important not to let anyone else make you feel ashamed for something that you don't think is shameful. If they find it awkward or embarrassing, that's their perception and possibly even their ignorance.

4 November

It's OK to say no for the sake of my mental health.

You can feel bad when you have to say no, but it can be necessary and the more you do it the easier it becomes! You need to maintain your boundaries and only take on what you can cope with. Don't worry about other people's disappointment – that's for them to manage.

I will help others to shine brighter.

I've noticed that a lot of people who have big followings on social media have been handing their accounts to lesser-known people who represent great causes. It allows those people to use their big platforms to shine a light on the issues they believe in. I love seeing people boost others and share their space! I know not everyone has millions of followers, but there are various ways in which we can help others to shine bright. Maybe you could tell some friends about someone who is doing great work or share about their cause on your social media?

6 November

Do an act of kindness: let a driver merge into your lane.

Driving is such a tense and fraught setting. I've found that people who are otherwise usually perfectly nice are horrible when they get behind the wheel or are waiting in traffic. If there's one place where acts of kindness are needed, it's on the road. How can you release some positivity on your travels today? Could you smile at other drivers, stop for pedestrians or be patient as the bus driver picks up passengers? Maybe, hardest of all, you could allow others to merge into your lane ahead of you or get on to the train before you? Give it a go. It could make travelling far more pleasant.

I will listen to my body.

Sometimes low self-esteem or, in its more extreme form, self-hatred, can stop us from tuning in to ourselves and our bodies. By observing ourselves, listening to how we're feeling, we can work out what will nourish our minds, souls and physical bodies, which will mean that we can look after ourselves much more effectively.

November

8 November

A heart at peace gives life
to the body,
but envy rots the bones.

Proverbs 14.30

We all know that jealousy and envy are very destructive. Any time you allow them to take over, in the end it's only you that you'll be punishing. It can become almost like a toxic juice swirling around your body, infecting your insides! Don't let it consume you – focus on being at peace and being kind to others instead.

Every morning, I have the opportunity to be a more joyful version of myself than I was yesterday.

Each day is a new start, like a blank page. Maybe yesterday was frustrating and you lost your temper while you were working or ran out of patience with your children – we all have those days! Today, you get to put that behind you and start again. Take a deep breath and focus on what brings you joy and how you might be able to bring a bit of joy to the lives of others.

November

10 November

I will not let my stress level break me.

When it comes to juggling work and family and everything else in life, it can be stressful. I know there are times when I feel that I just want to curl up in a ball in bed and never come out again! When everything hits at once, I find that taking a deep breath and saying out loud, 'I will not let my stress level break me,' gives me the strength to keep going. It is possible to have a lot on but not feel stressed.

11 November

Do what is right, not what is easy.

Roy T. Bennett

(*The Light in the Heart*, self-published, 2020)

Ultimately, I have to ask myself, 'Do you want to have things you want or do you want to be a person of integrity?' I would *like* to have a quiet life, but sometimes that's the easy route and facing a problem head on is the right thing to do. We have choices to make every single day and I am a great believer in sticking to your morals for each one. Is there a decision you need to make today between the easy route and the right one? Stand strong for what you believe in!

12 November

Sometimes rejection is protection.

I know only too well how much it hurts to be rejected. It's so important, though, for us to accept that rejection is a possibility every time we put ourselves out there. Then there's the horrible realization that just because you've come through the pain of rejection before, doesn't mean that you will escape having to do it again. A lot of the time, when I've been rejected in my life, I've realized with hindsight that the thing I've been turned down for or turned away from wasn't right for me at all. Then I just feel grateful after all that those doors were closed to me!

No act of kindness, no matter how small, is ever wasted.

In my life, I remember the big, monumental things that people have done for me, but also the small acts of kindness. I mean the *really* small things, like holding a door open or putting the kettle on. They're so everyday that the people won't even remember doing them! In this way, your impact can be way larger than you realize, because you won't always know how much that tiny thing meant to someone else.

14 November

I am not what I've done or been through; I am what I've conquered and overcome.

Don't let what has happened in your past affect how you approach things in your future. The fact is, pain builds resilience, patience and empathy in us. There's no space for shame in your life – celebrate the person your past has turned you into today!

I don't need to perform for other people.

As a woman, I have felt pressured to continually appease other people. At times, we women can try to please and placate and perform and have it all – I'm exhausted just thinking about it! We often look to others for approval or confirmation that we're getting it right, but the bottom line is that when you're living to please others, you are not really living. Because I am a Christian, I believe that my only guide should be God. I shouldn't care about pleasing others and need to remember that I'm living for an audience of one. How can your choices reflect who you are living for today?

16 November

In three words, I can sum up everything I've learned about life: it goes on.

Robert Frost

(In Ray Josephs, 'Robert Frost's secret', *The Cincinnati Enquirer*, Section: This Week Magazine, 5 September 1954)

If I had to pick one affirmation that summed up my whole life, I think it would be this one! There are so many challenges I've faced that I would have seen as life-ending when I was younger — some of them trivial and others far more serious. As time passes, though, I have come to realize that, no matter how hard things get, life goes on.

I will not hold a grudge.

One of the biggest areas of my own personal growth since I was younger has been reflecting on what really matters in life. I have given up holding grudges against people and making them suffer. The fact is, we will all do something to make the people we love feel bad from time to time. Not one of us is perfect! I believe that such situations can be used to strengthen relationships, but this has to start with forgiveness.

18 November

Look for the helpers and you will always find people who are helping.

Fred Rogers

Whenever there's a disaster reported in the news, I always try not to concentrate on the crime or the destruction but on the people who show up to help out. It can feel overwhelming when you focus on the pain, but when you see the selflessness of those who help, it's heart-warming. Even in our day-to-day lives, we can choose to focus on the pain point or on those friends, family, colleagues or sometimes strangers offering to lend a hand.

19 November

I will not compare my life to other people's curated social media output.

For some people, the only insight you get into their lives is what they show you on social media. I don't know if you find this, but I can start to build up an impression of them in my own mind that is actually just an edit or a photoshopped version of them. It's important to remember that a social media account is just fiction and not let it affect how you feel about yourself.

20 November

**Trust in the Lᴏʀᴅ with all your heart
and lean not on your
own understanding;
in all your ways, submit to him
and he will make your paths straight.**

Proverbs 3.5–6

I find that, at times, I overthink things and drive myself insane!
Over time, I've learnt that it is often the wrong approach,
because the answer doesn't always lie within myself.
Acknowledging that I can't solve everything with my own
understanding is great for easing anxiety. What 'uncontrollable'
thing can you let go of today?

My relationship (or hope for a relationship) doesn't complete me – I'm already whole.

I've found that it's so dangerous to want to fall in love in order to complete yourself. It's far better to work on yourself first, then bring that fuller version of you to a relationship with another person. That message is important to me even now that I'm in a relationship. I don't like to think of my husband as my 'other half' – I'm complete in my own right. Don't forget, it's not up to your partner to make you happy. It's up to you and your faith to make you feel whole.

22 November

I am not afraid to speak about my own achievements.

I've found that, like a lot of women, I can be scared to speak up. We don't want to look stupid or sound boastful. There have been many occasions when I've been interviewing women with a view to them joining our team at the Katie Piper Foundation and they've played down their achievements. I've even googled some candidates after the interview and only then seen how incredible they are! The men I interview are often very happy to sell themselves and highlight their strengths. Don't be afraid to wear your achievements like a badge of honour. Of course, you are not your achievements, but you don't need to belittle them!

23 November

I will live every day to the fullest.

I remember being at a seminar once and someone came on stage and said, 'Do you know when people really start living? When they're dying.' It was a bit of a morbid thought, but also really challenging. Every day that we are here is a gift, but we can get so caught up in the day-to-day that we forget that. What could you do today to experience life to the fullest?

24 November

Do an act of kindness: write to tell someone about the impact they've had on your life.

When I was experiencing my darkest moments, I was fortunate to have a handful of incredible people to help me piece things back together. Of course, you don't need to have been in a really desperate place to recognize that some people have had a profound and positive influence on you. Maybe it was a teacher or someone who looked after you, a great boss or someone who said just the right thing at the right time? Could you write them a message to let them know how pleased you are that they had that impact on your life? What a wonderful message that would be for them to receive!

Loneliness is and always has been the central and inevitable experience of every man.

Thomas Wolfe

To some the idea that we're all going to experience loneliness is a bit defeatist and depressing, but I find it liberating. I'm pleased that this reality is acknowledged, because even the most connected of people *will* experience loneliness from time to time. We don't need to be afraid of it and we definitely don't need to be embarrassed to admit it. The lovely irony is, if you're feeling lonely, you're not alone!

26 November

I will inhale love and exhale hate.

Filling yourself with love and actively choosing to breathe it into your body will help you to develop empathy for those around you. There's no need to bring hate into your mind and body. If I ever do allow it to creep in, I just remember that there's no need to keep it there! I just breathe in love and compassion, and breathe out the negative bits.

It's OK for someone to let me down; I'm strong enough to cope with it.

I have to remind myself regularly that I am far stronger than I realize. Being let down is inevitable, but we all have an inner strength to withstand it, whether we know it or not! You've built an endurance that is greater than you know. When things are really overwhelming me, I take some quiet time, recharge and tap into that inner strength.

28 November

Fear has a large shadow but he himself is small.

J. Ruth Gendler

(*The Book of Qualities*, Harper Perennial, 1988)

We can allow scary and difficult situations to grow into something massive in our minds. When I feel afraid, I like to break down the situation so I can get to the crux of what is causing my fear. Once I know that, I often feel less afraid. If we don't address this, it can turn into a huge shadow over our ambitions and our lives but fear isn't all that big when you look it in eye and bring it down to size.

I will not be afraid of difficulties.

Some of us have been conditioned to fear the dark times and avoid situations that we think will bring us pain. If my experiences have taught me anything, it's that the dark times are when we develop resilience – it's never built up when life is going well. Sadly, it's not a course you can sign up to online. The reality is that out of these difficulties can often come our greatest strength.

30 November

The people who get on in this world are the people who get up and look for the circumstances they want, and if they can't find them, make them.

George Bernard Shaw

(Mrs Warren's Profession, 1893)

Sometimes there are naysayers who feel so bound by their limitations that they spend all their time thinking about what *can't* be done. Instead of focusing on limitations and complaining about unachievable dreams, why not be one of the people Shaw writes about in his play, and put your energy into trying to achieve your dream? Self-belief is a great place to start!

December

1 December

If we had no winter, the spring would not be so pleasant. If we did not sometimes taste of adversity, prosperity would not be so welcome.

Anne Bradstreet

('Meditations Divine and morall', XIV, in John Harvard Ellis (ed.), *The Works of Anne Bradstreet in Prose and Verse*, Peter Smith, 1962)

We all want the good times, but if life were *all* good times, I don't know if I would be capable of fully appreciating and enjoying it. It is by comparing our dark times with our best that we realize how much we should treasure the moments of prosperity. This thought brings me so much hope when I am struggling, because I know I won't always be in that place and, when I'm not, I'll appreciate it even more.

December

2 December

The hardest thing about 'everything happens for a reason' is waiting for that reason to show up.

Attributed to Karen Salmansohn

I'm not a fan of the saying 'everything happens for a reason' on its own. I find the affirmation above far more realistic. On my own journey, I've found that it's easier to understand experiences with hindsight, and it's often when we look back that we can make sense out of them. With that in mind, if you're waiting to make sense of something now, I want you to find this hopeful. There is a struggle, and you may not understand it now, but you will in time.

3 December

I will not be afraid of saying the wrong thing.

We are often taught that getting things wrong is shameful. We can be afraid that if we don't manage to express ourselves in the most articulate way, we will sound stupid and people won't want to listen to us. Sometimes we even sit back and allow others to talk for us, not asserting ourselves because we don't want to make a fuss. It's so important that you know your voice is valuable, so never be afraid to speak out!

4 December

I will not judge the present moments based on the past.

It's so easy to live in fear and expect the worst — especially if you've faced trials in the past. I could easily lock myself away and never want to walk outside for fear of what could happen, but I know that would be such a shame. I don't want to be someone who judges all the present moments based on the past and I definitely don't want to pass that mentality on to my children. We can't wrap ourselves or our loved ones in cotton wool; we have to allow things to happen and trust that we will handle hardship with courage and strength.

5 December

I can listen and support without having to solve.

Often, what's needed in a situation isn't for us to try to fix people and solve problems. While strategizing has its place, what's more important is that the person feels heard. It's natural to try to give someone a solution when you see that person hurting, but sometimes it's better simply to acknowledge that it can be tough. Can you lend someone a listening ear today?

6 December

Know, first, who you are; and then adorn yourself accordingly.

Epictetus

Understanding your identity is such an important foundation
on which to build your life. As a Christian, I believe in God
as the Father, which means that my father is a king and I am
his child, a princess. I adorn myself with my crown every
morning and see myself as royalty – because that's
what I am! What beliefs are foundational
to who you are?

7 December

I will see each day as a gift and take nothing for granted.

I've known what it feels like not to be sure if today will be my last. For me, the memory of those times is a daily reminder that each day is a gift. Don't wait for disaster to strike before you realize how precious everything in your life is. Is there anything or anyone you're taking for granted?

8 December

I only fail when I stop trying.

Giving up on something feels so final to me. It takes a lot for me to walk away from something I'm passionate about. I always say, 'While I'm alive, I'm still going!' Is there a project or maybe even a person you may have given up on too quickly?

Don't say anything on social media that you wouldn't want *everyone* to see.

My agent always warns me not to say something that I wouldn't want to be a headline on the cover of a newspaper! When I want to say something out of anger or frustration, I ask myself if it represents me well enough to be in print. Sometimes the answer is no, so I have to hold my tongue! It's a really good litmus test for how we speak to others, both online and in person. Often those who post nasty comments online aren't terrible people, they've just got caught up in the moment and they feel safe behind the anonymity of the platform, but words hurt. They can hurt the person and reputations. Make sure you only say things you're proud of.

December

10 December

I don't have to relate to every motivational quote on the Internet.

I've found that positive quotes can rile me up if they're not well thought through. What good does it do, telling someone to 'get up and run with the sunshine on your face' if they've been in an accident and are unable to walk? Not everyone has the option to 'seize the day'. If that's where you're at, then that's OK. Ignore the well-meant 'motivation' and know that you're doing your best and your best is more than enough.

I will stand up and speak up for my rights.

We all have fundamental rights – or, at least, we should do. Injustice is all around us on this Earth. Unfortunately, it's often the least, the last and the lost – those who don't have a strong voice – who suffer most. That means if you don't fall into that category, maybe you can do something to stand up for someone else who doesn't have the chance for their voice to be heard. When the strongest stand up and shout loud, those who are weaker gain their strength.

12 December

. . . we can comfort those in any trouble with the comfort we ourselves receive from God.

2 Corinthians 1.3–4

The idea that God is so interested in comforting us is (and perhaps unsurprisingly) a real comfort to me! I like to think that God is out there restoring the broken-hearted and those who are in trouble. It also inspires me to reach out a comforting hand to those around me. Whether you feel full of faith right now or not, who can you provide comfort to today?

I will choose to engage with the content that fulfils me.

I try really hard not to endlessly scroll through social media feeds, but when I slip up and find myself doing this (which I definitely do from time to time), I can feel myself getting irritable and fed up. What I've realized is, when I engage in things that aren't real and don't fulfil me, it lowers my mood and makes me feel that I have no direction. Better to focus on what's real and important to me, like the people I care about!

14 December

Do an act of kindnes: always pass on a good book.

When you finish a good book, it can feel amazing — as if you've learnt something you never would have otherwise or you've been transported into another world or life. I love getting books as gifts from my friends because it means that they were thinking of me, but also it means that they have hand-picked something they think I will love. Is there a book you've enjoyed recently that you could pass on to a friend?

15 December

I will invest in my family — whatever family looks like for me.

When I talk about 'family', I don't necessarily think of a biological family. Some people have that 'traditional' set-up, but others build their family from a group of friends and some find family in their community groups or support groups or churches or other religious institutions. Whatever family looks like for you, it's important to invest in the people you care about most and who care about you.

16 December

A ship in harbour is safe but that is not what ships are built for.

John A. Shedd

Nothing can grow if it's kept wrapped up and out of danger. This fact is key for me when I think about my children. They are so precious that I just want to hold them tight and not let them out into the world, but how much life and adventure would they miss out on if I did that? The best parents raise their children so that, one day, they don't need them. In time, we all have to venture out on our own and learn from our own experiences.

I will reframe my problems as opportunities.

We've all heard the familiar affirmation that when one door closes, another door opens. I almost didn't want to include it in this book because it's a bit of an obvious one, but it's popular because it's true. Don't let 'problems' get you down. There may be an incredible opportunity waiting for you on the other side.

December

18 December

I will not pretend to be something I'm not.

I've found so much freedom in doing this. I know that I am loved by my friends, family and God and, through that, I've learnt to love myself. I don't need to hide who I am from anyone. Do you find yourself pretending to be something you're not in order to be liked? Maybe it's time to stop pretending and embrace the real you!

19 December

Comparison is the thief of joy.

Attributed to Theodore Roosevelt

No one can ever know the reality of someone else's life. I have been known to look at people's social media or meet people for a moment and make assumptions about what their lives are like but, in fact, all I can see is a snippet of how that person lives. I've realized that, ultimately, I'm comparing myself to something that actually doesn't exist. Don't lose your joy or your peace by chasing something that's not real anyway!

20 December

I can't control everything that happens, but I can control how I respond.

I don't agree with the classic saying, 'Life is what you make it.' Some things are out of your control and others happen to you that you couldn't have influenced with positivity or by changing your behaviour. Knowing that you can control some things and identifying those in difficult moments, though, can be key. In the end, you are in control of how you respond to trials, how you store up negative things and how long you allow them to live, rent free, in your mind.

21 December

I will not be held back by 'weakness'.

The best example of this I can think of is when you see a paralympian. I know a lot of them dislike the word 'disabled', because they're able to do so much, they just find another route. I'm really inspired by their capability in a world not designed to accommodate them. Is there anything that you see as a weakness when, in fact, you just need to find another route?

22 December

Never stop doing your best because someone doesn't give you credit.

It is so annoying when someone doesn't credit you for your idea or achievement. The driving force behind what we do, though, shouldn't be the recognition we think that it will get us. When I'm feeling that I should receive more praise, I have to step back and ask myself what my motive was when I started. Often the answer isn't that I wanted the credit but that I wanted to achieve something or help out.

23 December

I will support those around me.

My parents were one of the inspirations behind me setting up my charity to help the survivors of burns and scars. When I really needed it, my parents provided a network of people I could connect with and a safe place for me to recover. At the charity, we work with those who have been injured but it often involves so much more than purely medical support. There are logistics to be worked out, paying rent and bills, doing a food shop and feeling able to leave the house and rejoin society again. My parents helped me with those things when I needed it most. Is there anyone you could reach out a helping hand to today?

December

24 December

May the God of hope fill you with all joy and peace as you trust in him, so that you may overflow with hope by the power of the Holy Spirit.

Romans 15.13

When I'm at a low point, the idea of overflowing with hope feels intangible at best and, at worst, impossible. In fact, we can all choose to hope, and cultivating hope is so important. That's what this season is all about for me. Hope for brighter days, hope for success at work or for your family to succeed. What can you hope for today?

25 December

It's the moments together that change us for ever.

In our house, Christmas is such a special time of togetherness. I know that for some this will be with family or a partner's family or with friends or church family but, whatever it looks like, I know that time is so precious. Everyone has different traditions today — for us it's board games and far too much chocolate! Whatever you get up to, I'm wishing you a very merry Christmas.

26 December

I will embrace new experiences.

Do you have a bucket list of fun things that you'd love to try before you 'kick the bucket'? Maybe you want to eat a food that you've never tasted or visit a new country or tell someone you love them or skydive out of a plane?! You can experience new things and live out your dreams right now.

So, what's on your list . . . ?

27 December

I can't be strong all the time and that's OK.

Not all difficult situations have a clear-cut or one solution. Sometimes the best thing you can do in the face of trials is to allow yourself to feel what you feel. I love a good cry from time to time – it's therapeutic! Allowing yourself to experience your emotions, instead of dumbing them down or trying to mask them, is a really healthy thing to do. Feeling something is being strong!

28 December

I will have a little bit of faith.

My faith in God grew out of a dark place of desperation. In that moment I heard him say to me, 'There is so much more than this. You're not alone. You're part of something much bigger.' Because I felt that he came just when I needed him, I never doubted that God was real. I know not everyone reading this will believe what I believe, and that's OK, but there is a freedom in having faith that there is so much more than your current pain, you are not alone and you're part of something much bigger than yourself.

What feels like the end is often the beginning.

Between Christmas and New Year is often a weird time. I know I can lose track of what day it is and feel a bit funny as I reflect on the year that's been. If you feel a little depressed after all the buzz and excitement of Christmas is over, don't despair! This is a great time to dream and scheme for the year ahead and to get in some R&R so that you're ready to dive into the New Year head first. Be kind to yourself today.

30 December

When you are tempted to get discouraged, remind yourself that according to God's word, your future is getting brighter; you are on your way to a new level of glory.

Joel Osteen

(*Your Best Life Now*, FaithWords, 2015)

In the winter months, we can long for the brighter times (both literally and metaphorically). I know I always think that I can't wait till things feel lighter again, in every sense. In those moments, I hold on to the idea that those brighter days will come, because they always do. Sometimes they'll come tomorrow and sometimes it will be a bit longer, but they *do* always come.

31 December

Nobody can go back and start a new beginning, but anybody can start today and make a new ending.

Attributed to Zig Ziglar

We all have so many beginnings and endings in life. How something started and how it progressed since then is all in the past, but you can change the course of that situation, starting right now. Is there a feud that's gone on too long? Something you feel you could have done better? Maybe you could extend an olive branch now or choose to do better from today. This affirmation, from American author and motivational speaker Zig Ziglar, reminds me that it's never too late to start again.

Acknowledgements

My first and biggest thank you goes to you, to every person who has faithfully bought and gifted my books, connected with me and generally cheered me on. I am constantly inspired by the stories I hear and the messages I receive from you. They push me forwards, to keep writing books like this one. You have all my love and gratitude. Thank you for being an ever-positive presence in my life.

I, of course, also need to offer a big shout out to those who get the 'not so positive' side of me but lift me up all the same: my best friend – my husband – my supportive family and my children. You are the daily tonic that makes me smile on the darkest of days.

Huge and heartfelt thank yous to my publishing team at SPCK – Elizabeth Neep, Michelle Clark and Sam Snedden – and to Lauren Windle for sharing my vision, believing in me and wanting to spread positivity. Thank you also to the team at Fresh Partners and Belle PR for being as passionate as I am about this project and always supporting me in all I do.

Last, but certainly not least, I want to thank every person who has engaged with my daily affirmations on social media. Sharing those snippets of hope with you throughout the global pandemic and subsequent national lockdowns made me feel so close to you all as we journeyed through such a strange and surreal time together. Many of you said that you wanted me to write a new book of affirmations and here it is – but it's not my book, it's *ours*, and I look forward to sharing these affirmations with you over the coming days, weeks and months.